CW01645364

Property Investment Survival Manual: "Six of the Best" Property Mistakes and Essential Lessons To Learn

Published by Touchstone Education LLP,
Duniera,
Pier Road Rhu,
G84 8LH

Table of Contents

Introduction: Welcome to My Book

Welcome to The Property Investment Survival Manual.

This book represents 50 years of my property investment experiences, from watching my Grandads and Dad through to doing our own projects.

My goal for you is simple: to help you earn more money in less time from property by learning from my experiences.

As long as you're motivated, implementation-minded and follow the systems I present for your business, you'll understand the concepts fast.

Here is what to expect of this book so you get the most out of it and your expectations are met:

First, it's interactive. There are lots of opportunities for you to go deeper into the content, gain access to free training videos, participate in free interactive masterclass events and more.

Second, this book is for your business. It's intended to help you grow your business, produce real results and make money quickly. A business is a profitable financial enterprise that works without you.

Third, it's for implementers. There are lots of learnings that you can use right now to grow your property business. If you're looking for free, easy money, this isn't the book for you.

Fourth, this book wasn't intended to be an Amazon #1 Bestseller, I have already written one of those. It's designed to start a conversation with you, give you and me a chance to get to know each other better, develop trust, a bond and ultimately help us decide if we will work together someday.

Fifth, this is a book packed with implementable content and lots of ideas. My intention and the purpose of this book is to show you the most powerful ways to invest in property, with as many safeguards as you can put in place. You'll notice there are opportunities throughout this book to watch free training videos and downloadable guides and YES, I do have some great further educational courses to make you more money. They work and I've helped many thousands of people with my educational programmes and I'm certain they'll help you too. I'd absolutely love to hear from you, get to know you better and see you post your success story, picture or video and comment on Facebook at www.facebook.com/PaulandAniko

The best way to start working with me is to visit the links in this book, join me for the training masterclass, and learn more about how to grow your property portfolio. It's my pleasure to help you make more money, change your life and gain more freedom!

Best regards,

Paul Smith

Rhu, Argyll and Bute, Scotland

Bonus Follow Up Tool

Visit **http://bit.ly/portfoliocallme** to get your "Building Your Property Portfolio" plan. See how to automate the process by texting **"CALL" to 01302 590 656**

Chapter One: Origins

I was born into a normal family. Both of my parents were teachers. My father was a headmaster and my mother was a primary school teacher. Going back another generation on my English side, I'm half-English and half-Irish, my paternal grandma was in service. She was a maid in a big house and my grandad was born to a family of dockers in Kent. He was considered to have done well because he became a tradesman, initially a carpenter and then a cabinet-maker. Perhaps in another book on another day I'll talk more fully about my grandad on my English side, and maybe I'll talk more fully about my grandad on my Irish side too.

During the early days of the Second World War, Grandma, Grandad and my Dad were living in Crystal Palace in London. This was before my Grandad joined the army. He volunteered because he felt that if he volunteered he'd perhaps have a better choice about what he actually wanted to do, as opposed to being told what to do. He was initially a regular in the infantry and then he joined the Corps of Engineers, which became the Royal Engineers. I think his trade background helped him in that regard.

Grandad impacted my life in a significant way. He helped me genuinely come to believe that absolutely anything is possible. The limitation on our achievement, I truly believe, is our imagination. If we can come to conceive, if we can imagine it and then believe that it's possible, we can achieve it. I truly believe that. I am not going to say that Grandad was humble, he was anything but humble, he was opinionated and could be hard on people. He was a strong man with strong views.

He spent six years in Asia-Pacific during the Second World War. During this time, Grandma and Dad were, as I said, living in Crystal Palace. Whilst they lived there the Blitz began, again that is a whole different story for a different day, but they lived in Crystal Palace throughout the Blitz. Ironically, they got evacuated to Yorkshire just as the Blitz was dying down, and there they lived with a family who kindly took them in for many of the war years.

What does that mean and why is it relevant to property investment? Well, for this reason. My English Grandad's name was Wilf, there's a good old English name, isn't it? Wilfred. Wilf came back from the war. He started off as a private and by the time he went away he was a sergeant. By the time he came back he was a full colonel. For those who know anything about ranks within the British military, that's a senior rank and there is no way during normal circumstances, especially then (though it might be a little bit different now), that a carpenter from Kent could end up as a colonel in the Engineers. No chance.

Here's where we get to the real nitty gritty. Obviously, there was no such thing as the internet then and Grandad couldn't send his money home even if he wanted to. Dad and Grandma were living with a very kind couple in Yorkshire. The family hadn't really needed money, so he came back with several years of senior officer's pay in cash, in his pocket.

He took his first step to financial freedom, to allow him to do what he wanted to do, by buying a field in Essex and building a bungalow on it. Although I was from a "normal family" it was also normal in my family that people go and build their own houses. He built that property in the late 1940's into the early 1950's and he lived in it for the rest of his days. He died at ninety-four and he never owned any property, apart from the one that he built.

Property has got a habit of giving and then keeping on giving. Many years after Grandad built his property, which was in a place called Little Thurrock in Grays in Essex, he was approached by the local county council who wanted to purchase some of his garden. We're rolling forward to the '70s now and I remember this because I was born in 1964 and in the mid-70s I was aware of what was going on. I was interested in business dealings by then, just like my children are now.

He hadn't needed planning permission to build his bungalow. All that sort of stuff Grandad considered "new-fangled", and he didn't really approve of such things. Somebody's got some land, they want to build a house, nothing to do with the government. He had massively strong views on things like that. He didn't like central authority. His mindset, his capabilities and his achievements demonstrated one thing above everything else; independence.

He didn't want some "bumbling bureaucrats", which is what he used to call them, (sorry if any local authority workers are listening to or reading this!) interfering with his family's legacy; his land. He fought for years to stop them buying his land.

Eventually, they used compulsory purchase to buy it off him and he hated that. It wasn't about the money, rather through compulsory purchase they took away a man's land, a man who had fought for this country. He hated that with an absolute passion. Ultimately, and this again is irony, that's what gave him his financial freedom. He took a good chunk of cash off the council in exchange for his acres which meant he never had to work a day again in his life. Instead, he returned to his roots. He went back to school and became a teacher and taught carpentry.

On every occasion I've ever known, when a person gets complete and absolute financial freedom they do what they actually want to do, what they were born to do. Despite the fact that by almost anyone's standards he was now a wealthy man, despite his rank in the army, despite his broad choice of careers and occupations he became a teacher. In many ways I regard myself as a third-generation teacher. My Grandad, my Mum and Dad, and now me.

I'll flip over to the other side of the Irish Sea now and talk about my Irish Grandad, and you couldn't get a more Irish name than his, PJ Flood. Patrick Joseph Flood. He also had his finger in the "property pie", but in a different way. My Irish Grandad, like many Irish people of his generation, was a farmer. He wasn't a landowner. Instead, he started life as a tenant farmer, minded his money, made some shrewd investments and ended up being able to buy a hotel. This particular one, his first, was Flood's Hotel in a place called Pettigo.

He was inspirational to me in so many ways. He was a pure commercial animal. Unfortunately, he died relatively young, in his sixties, so I never got to know him as well as my English Grandad. I do remember Patrick Joseph, or Paddy as he was called, but they are early childhood memories. I never had the deep discussions with him that I had with my English Grandad, as I was only five or six when PJ passed away.

My English Grandad taught me to play chess, taught me to argue and taught me to be clear about what I wanted and why I wasn't going to let anybody else take my things, my thoughts or my reputation from me. He gave me a great gift: Independence of mind and spirit, and I thank him for it.

I can't really give you a detailed commentary about how and when Paddy passed away because I was too young. We shouldn't live our lives in regret. Had I been even slightly older when he passed away, another five or ten years perhaps, I'm certain I would have been involved in his business. He owned several hotels, pig farms, stud farms and thousands of acres of land. He had a proper business empire and a number of different independent streams of income, all made possible by one thing. His greatest achievement was that he became the local auctioneer which meant any time anything got sent to auction, he had the first pick. He got to know the "movers and shakers" and he got to know the land owners and the wealthy people, and they all talked to him because he was the auctioneer.

He spent his early life cutting the turf in the bogs. In the part of Ireland that my family are from to this day they still burn turf. As he moved himself out of those humble beginnings, in a different but equally admirable way to my English Grandad, he developed business skills and acumen because he associated with smart people. Everybody's heard the expression, your network is your net worth, but how many of us actually spend good chunks of time building on our network? Virtually none of us. If PJ, was anything, he was a professional networker.

I don't know for sure but maybe that's where I get my love of networking, talking to people, public performance. I genuinely love it. Some people fear public speaking. For some it is higher on their list of things that they don't want to do than death! I'm quite an unusual person in this regard, and I'm going to credit my Irish Grandad with that.

In different ways my family were in the "property business": property through self-build and compulsory purchase of acres on the English side and hotels, land, pig farms and stud farms through an auctioneering business on the Irish side. Very different types of property business but both generated very significant wealth in just a single generation. Now you might thinking, okay Paul, you're effectively telling us that you were born with a "silver spoon in your mouth". Well actually no. PJ passed away young and being an Irish catholic he had nine sons and daughters, many of which did extraordinary things, but some of which took extraordinary amounts of his money, his legacy away.

He did leave a substantial estate. However, because it was divided by so many people and because there was nobody, and this isn't a criticism, in the family that was business orientated, the wealth that was grown in a single generation was lost in about half a generation. His children were family orientated but didn't have business acumen. One of his sons, for instance, PJ junior, was very athletic. He played Gaelic Football for Donegal, who have only ever won the All-Ireland Gaelic Football Championships twice. The first time they did, PJ, my uncle, was in the team. Plenty of high achievers in so many ways but there was nobody there with the business drive that Grandad possessed.

On my English side, my Grandma and Grandad fortunately lived to a ripe old age. Grandad passed away at the age of ninety-four. He had a fantastic life with all sorts of colourful incidents, all the way through the Second

World War and not forgetting the fights that he had with the council (and many other organisations!). He never had a sick day in his life until the day he had a heart attack, and even then, he did it perfectly. It was the first time he'd ever been in hospital. They said to him, 'Mr Smith, we think you've got between two and three days to live,'. He said, 'splendid, bring all the family in. I can say goodbye to them and then I'll die.' That is exactly what he did. A life well-lived.

As soon as he passed away, something broke inside my Grandma. Every time I saw her she would tell me all her friends were dead, brothers and sisters were dead, her husband was dead. She was just waiting to die. Her health deteriorated, and she went into a care home. My Mum in particular spent years looking after her and Grandma died at ninety-nine and a half years old. If there's a more efficient mechanism for burning wealth that exists on this planet than care and nursing homes then I don't know what it is. Very few things can destroy wealth more quickly than end of life care.

This is what destroyed a significant chunk of my English family's wealth. What was left was passed on to my dad and his sister. Again, neither of them were particularly business, investment or finance orientated. Dad couldn't care less about money. He only cared about one thing, education and educating people. Reading, learning, knowledge. The day my father died he was actually writing a book about Alexander the Great and some specific technical details on weaponry of the age.

So, that's my formative years and what property meant to me. I could see that on both sides of my family property had generated wealth and I'd also seen that unless it's protected by trusts, pensions and pension schemes, it has a propensity, like the tide, to fall just as rapidly as it rises. I was attracted to property investment, I knew it could generate wealth, but I wanted to understand how that wealth could become legacy and transgenerational, which is a very different thing.

In the next chapter I'm going to move on to my childhood years and I'm going to go forward a generation, from my grandparents to my parents. Don't forget, this book isn't a property "get-rich-quick" tome. This book is a no-holds-barred, "behind-the-scenes" manual. I'll show you the good stuff, of course, but I'm actually more focused in this instance on showing you the bad stuff, the mistakes that I've made and the mistakes I've seen others make.

This books subtitle "Six of the Best Property Mistakes and Essential Lessons to Learn" is a tribute to my Father, a headmaster. In his time, headmasters routinely used to cane pupils or "give them the belt". One of the things I'm proudest of about my father is that he educated thousands of students for all those years and never did he resort to "Six of the Best". His love of learning was extraordinary this book is for him. "He who never made a mistake never made anything..." I can hear his voice now. Well Dad I made plenty and I want to do what you did, help others to learn.

In the next chapter, we are moving on from my grandparents' generation to my parents and my early childhood.

Chapter Two: The Early Years

It still feels surreal to me that these days as well as reading books I write them. I've got to say, I love it. Einstein once said, "There comes a point in your life when you need to stop reading other people's books and write your own." I'm so very pleased that I have been able to take that advice.

In my early years we moved house, typically every two or three years. As I mentioned in the previous chapter, both my parents were teachers. This meant, amongst other things, that they didn't earn very much money. That's not to say that my childhood was bad, it wasn't, it was great, absolutely fabulous. The freedom to roam safely, fields and open spaces, books and a loving environment. I spent my primary school years in two towns in Yorkshire; Hemsworth and Wombwell.

So, here's what my Mum and Dad would do. They would typically buy quite a big, old, Victorian house and they would improve it. What does 'improve' mean, in this sense? For a start, Dad would always electrically re-wire it. Just to give you the context on this, he was a history teacher but he was also the son of a Royal Engineer, he was the son of a carpenter. I am pretty sure you've all heard this expression before: 'If you think you can, or think you can't, you're probably right.' He watched his Dad building that bungalow in Essex. My Dad, although he was a history teacher and subsequently headmaster, thought it was entirely normal for anybody to re-wire a house. He got a book, read it, got somebody to give him some information, some advice, got some education, got some tuition, got some support, and just started wiring houses in his spare time.

What else did he do? Install central heating! So, an electrician, a plumber and what would be called a heating engineer now. He would do it himself, from scratch, everything. Absolutely everything and I would help him do it. After the plumbing, often creating indoor toilets to replace the outside one the houses often had, and wiring it would be plastering, painting and then the finishing touches.

A house that I remember very clearly is the second one that we refurbished in Wombwell. I remember going under the floorboards there because I was smaller than Dad then. I was quite large for my age. I haven't grown a millimetre since the age of eleven when I reached six-foot-tall! So, I don't think I would describe myself as small but I was smaller than Dad, more agile and then either eight or nine years old. I've got vivid, vivid memories of going under the floorboards on the first and second floor. This particular property was a three storey one and a cellar as well. What was my job? Under the floorboards pulling out all of the old lead wiring and lead pipes. None of the modern wiring and plumbing you would see today. I was literally pulling out lead wiring and lead plumbing. At the age of eight I was using power-tools. Chopping it up and ripping it out and I loved it! Wombwell was in a mining area and I used to come up looking like a coal-miner. It was almost like I'd done a shift by the time I came up from under the floorboards. I am so grateful I had few limits as a child. I am sure experiences like this freed my mind to take on new-challenges. Not many parents today would allow the eight year old Paul to do what he did. "Health and Safety" are ingrained into so much of what children are restricted from doing. I know the intent is good, I am not so sure the result is equally beneficial.

I learned then that property can pay you in all sorts of different ways. As a child I didn't understand mortgages and mortgage finance and what my parents were doing with the money that they were releasing. Nor did I understand the fact that there was no capital gains when you refurbished your home, increased its value, and then sold it again.

I should not assume that everybody understands the huge financial benefits dad was achieving with these refurbished houses and the fact that you can still do this today.

Buy a relatively cheap, dated and tired property then refurbish it so that it is worth a lot more money and sell it, there's no tax at all on that extra cash you release. Happy days. I didn't know all that. What did property mean to me in the early days? It meant this. Every Saturday we'd get the wheelbarrow and me and Dad would fill it up with all the metal that I'd stripped that week unless it was more than a wheelbarrow load. We just did one wheelbarrow every Saturday. I used to love chatting to Dad as we pushed my lovely metal up to the scrap-yard. The money that we got for it I could keep. Imagine that. Lead wiring, lead plumbing, copper off-cuts. So property in the early years became my pocket money. Happy days indeed!

My Dad trained himself as an electrician and he trained himself as a plumber. This wasn't luck. This wasn't chance, it was his choice. He did this whilst having a busy job and bringing up me and my two brothers and sister. So, what else did he do to our homes? It was a bit early for double glazing, so we didn't generally do that, but we sometimes changed a few windows. The other thing we almost always had to do was put in some extra bathrooms because typically in these sorts of properties the bathrooms were outside in the yard. It definitely wasn't a question of "all mod-cons". When we moved into these properties they typically had no central-heating, they had coal fires, outside toilets and really, really, dodgy wiring. In fact, in the Wombwell house I talked about, one of the things I had to rip out was all of the gas pipes. By the time we got there they weren't operational because the house was equipped for gas lighting which hadn't been used for years.

At my age I couldn't appreciate how and why my parents were doing it. I knew that they were doing it, after all I was helping them do it. It was normal for me that even though Dad was a headmaster, he was also a plumber, electrician and joiner, quite happy putting in a new bathroom, tiling, painting and decorating. He did everything himself. Much though I respected him for it that is not my approach today. For me to do all the hands-on work myself would be inefficient because the hourly rate I can achieve by doing what I do, webinars, courses, educating and writing books, is higher than the hourly rate I pay to very good tradespeople. Therefore, it makes no financial sense for me to do that. It's all about mindset.

What did working with my Father teach me? He taught me, and showed me, that anything is possible. He demonstrated to me, on a practical basis, that a man of books, a man of words, an educated man, can learn trades and very proficiently execute all the strategies associated with being a tradesman. Why was he arrogant enough to believe he could do all these things? Well, he was the son of a tradesman. He was a working-class boy, bombed during the Blitz. He moved with his Mum to Yorkshire, living all on their own for years. He became the "Man of the House" at a very young age and he did incredible things. My Mum gave him unwavering support. She would look after all the children all of the time without a word of complaint whilst me, being the eldest, and my Dad would be crashing about with hammers and drills and anything else nosey I could find!

Financially it got tight sometimes. It happens when you're doing a refurb. I could see that my parents needed extra cash. My Mum would also support the family financially too.

I remember once Mum took me over to Doncaster, not far from where Touchstone Educations main UK office is now, it's one of the reasons we chose Doncaster for our head-office. We went to somebody's house and Mum told me we were going to "a party" and another word I did not understand at that point. I thought, a party, hooray! Balloons, cake, clowns, that sort of thing. But when we arrived there was not a balloon, a cake, or even a "tooter" in sight.

Mum had taken me on the bus and we'd taken two huge empty suitcases with us each. What's all this about, I thought? Why am I going to a party with my Mum, but my brothers and sister aren't coming? Why is Dad not coming? Why am I on my own? By this time, I was almost eleven, a big boy at around six-foot-tall. I ended up sitting in a room where every single other person in that room was the same age as my Mum, or older, and they were all female. I thought, this is not my idea of a party, but okay, what's going to happen here? One of the women got up, in her front room, and started showing off bits of plastic. Boxes with lids on and similar stuff. What? This is a party?

Halfway through, Mum sent me out to the kitchen to open a few bottles of wine. It was the sort of wine that was considered "fancy" back then. I'm talking about the 1970's now, so it was really classy Blue Nun and similar vintage offerings. I had to take the corks out, which was another new skill I had to learn that day, operating a cork-screw, I'd never done that before. Then take trays of glasses back into the other room. There must have been thirty women in there, packed around the hostess, and she did something I'd never seen in my life before. The hostess did a sales pitch. Mum got all excited. A couple of gulps of Liebfraumilch, or whatever it was, and she made her decision. 'Get them suitcases, Paul. This is the opportunity of a lifetime.' I had never seen so much money. Out of Mum's purse came rolls and rolls of cash. Suddenly, we were officially Tupperware agents. I can't actually remember if we got a badge or anything, but they made you feel really special. It was something that I was fascinated by from that day forward. I love sales.

If I am selling a quality product or service that the client needs and they do not buy from me, I feel that I have failed them. I know that knowledge came from my experience with Mum at that Tupperware "party".

So another lesson in commerce for me. Nothing to do with property this time, but Mum was backwards and forwards with me on the bus with those suitcases. Mum got very good, very fast, at selling Tupperware and I was her assistant. In the evenings during the week, Mum would run Tupperware parties from the house and my job was to run around looking after the women, chatting them up, I was getting to that age where I could. I would serve glasses of whatever we had, Black Tower, Liebfraumilch, Blue Nun. This was not top of the range wine, but it was for it's time. It was thought to be very swanky, very, you know, posh where we lived.

My early years were a combination of helping Dad with physical work and Mum with sales. I have to say, in every way I loved it. Moving through my early teenage years it was more of the same. Dad was promoted from being a deputy to being a headmaster, which meant a move all the way down south from Yorkshire to Hertfordshire. We moved to a place called Hatfield in Hertfordshire, and, as we always did, we bought a house that needed compete modernisation. I was now old enough now to understand far more about the whole transaction.

The particular house that we bought was, yet again, a three-storey Victorian property with seven bedrooms and a cellar. It needed rewiring and re-plumbing and this time we actually put double glazing in too! This house already had two inside bathrooms, but we put a third one in. By now, I was developing my handyman skills. I'm still not great but I can plaster and I can paint. So as well as ripping everything out and getting the cash for that, I would also get an hourly rate from Dad for doing whatever he needed me to do. Obviously, he wouldn't pay me anything like a normal tradesman would get but he taught me I could exchange my time for money. Much more valuable was this lesson: You've only got a finite amount of time, and you can only sell that time once and you're not getting it back.

Wealthy people do not exchange time for money. They have learned to make money while they sleep.

My parents bought the house for £11,000. The total refurbishment cost was under £5,000 as we did all of the work ourselves. They sold it and moved house again when I was eighteen years old for £65,000. Over a period of seven years they turned £16,000 into £65,000. They quadrupled their money in seven years which is a fabulous return on investment. Even better it was tax free because it was our home.

For the first time I can ever remember they had spare money because they did not reinvest every penny into another house to redevelop. Dad had just got a new job as a headmaster at a bigger school and they moved to Bushey, near Watford. As part of the package he got a house to live in for a very affordable rent. I never lived in that house with them as I had left home by then. They could afford a decent car, holidays and really started to enjoy life which was great to see after so many years of their hard work.

These are my early years and my last memories before I became a property investor myself. I left home for college at seventeen to do my first degree which was a sponsored degree. I'm certain my parents gave me the motivation to do that.

Nobody in the family on either side had ever been to university before Dad. He really brought education to our family and he made it massively important for all of us.

Very early in his life he decided he wanted to go to university however he failed his "11 Plus" so didn't manage to get into a grammar school. He put his head down, vowed that that wasn't going to happen to him ever again and he passed his "13 Plus". He attended Grays Grammar School for Boys in Essex. From there he got into St Catherines college at Oxford University.

Once more: 'If you think you can or you think you can't, you're probably right.' Time after time my family has proven to me that if you set your heart on a goal, if you set your mind on something, you can do it. There's only one thing that stops you from achieving whatever it is you want to achieve, and that one thing? It's normally You.

We're now at the end of my early years. I have learned my English Grandad did a new build, sell off acres to the council under compulsory purchase and make them pay through the nose for it. I have learned my Irish Grandad built up a multi-faceted commercial property empire, hotels, farms, farmland, horses, pigs, all sorts of things, as a result of being a local auctioneer. My Dad going to university the first in his family, massively reinforcing the importance of education. "Working class boy" goes to Oxford University. I have seen my Mum start an entrepreneurial business, Tupperware, to supplement our family income. All of this is normal to me.

I have seen my parents, time after time, buy an old Victorian house, do it up and sell it for more money. After all the years of financial struggle, just as I left home, I saw Mum and Dad enjoying the financial rewards for all their hard work, all during my early years.

I was now ready to go out into the world. What did Paul do next? The next chapter is 'First Steps.' If you're not a property investor yet, you're going to be particularly interested in this because all I've given you so far are my formative influences, why I thought like I did, why I think like I think.

'First Steps', is particularly relevant to you if you're thinking about 'How do I learn about this stuff?' 'What should I do first?'.

Well, you've taken a great first step, you've actually bought this book and you are reading it or, potentially, listening to it. So well done and thank you, I'll see you in the next chapter.

Chapter Three: First Steps

My Mother, through all the years I was growing up, used to get the Co-op man to come to the door. She would initially give him four pence, then six pence and then a full shilling. During these years they had very, very little spare money, she would save a little for each of us children. By the time it came for me to leave home and go off to university she said to me, 'Paul, before you go I want you to have this.' She gave me £250. I was stunned. This was just before selling the house in Hatfield made them a lot of money, they didn't earn a lot. Mum did Tupperware part-time, Dad was a teacher and they had four kids. There had been nothing spare at the end of every month.

I had never had this much money before. "What's this?" I asked. 'That's the Co-op money,' said Mum. She'd been paying into a little savings plan since I was born so that I had something to go out into the world with. Because I knew it was so important to her, my promise to myself was that whatever I did, I would not waste that money. I would do something valuable with it. I put it in a savings account and I vowed it wasn't coming out until I had a good use for it. £250 pounds was a huge amount of money for me. I wanted to think carefully about what to use my money for. I also wanted to make sure that me going in university wasn't a financial burden or a strain on my family.

It had been a possibility that I would go to Oxford or Cambridge. I did the "Oxbridge" entrance exams a year before my "A levels" and I received an offer from St Catherine's Oxford. What a surprise.... I didn't like it for two reasons. Firstly my offer was far lower than the normal two A's and a B that other people would have received. They were making it very easy for me to go to Oxford. Why? Simply because my Dad went there. This wasn't fair and I knew my English Granddad wouldn't have liked it. The second reason was that if I went there and paid for halls of residence and everything else, I knew it would cost my parents a lot of money. In hindsight I am pretty sure that is why they did not buy another house. They were preparing to put us children through University.

I was determined to look for more suitable options for myself for university. I wasn't anti-university, I was just anti paying a fortune for university. The other consideration at that precise time was Margaret Thatcher. In all sorts of ways I do admire her and she reminds me strongly of my English Granddad. That said I was about to become a student and Mrs Thatcher was in the process of removing student grants. I didn't want to be holding out my hands to my parents for money all the time. They had worked really hard their entire lives for the money they now had. I needed to find some other option that was better for me and better for them.

'The quality of the questions you ask determines the quality of answers you get, and in turn that determines the quality of your life.'

The question I asked myself was:

"How can I get paid to go to university and whilst there, how can I have living costs of virtually zero?"

I found a two-part answer to this question. Part one: How do I get paid to go to university? Well, I was determined to find myself a sponsored university degree. This was in the August of that year and the term was starting at the end of September and I was just about starting to look. I rapidly narrowed it down to two universities.

Actually, it was one university, Aston, and one polytechnic, North East London Polytechnic, and they both offered courses in "Manufacturing Studies", mainly engineering. Aston University was quickly ruled out as they had just filled their last place. So North-East London Polytechnic it was, although it's now a university. I don't understand why they had to turn all the polytechnics into universities, I was happy with the technology colleges. I booked my interview and a few days later off I went.

Their academic requirements were very simple. I needed at least two E's at A level. I thought that was easy!

They said "No, no, no, Paul. You've been accepted by the university" (or by the polytechnic as it was then), "but that doesn't mean you're coming here. We only accept students if they're sponsored as well. We've got two sponsorship places left for this year: one is with Plessy Radar, and the other is with the Ford Motor Company."

I said, 'Hmm, okay, I need to think about it. I'll let you know which one I'm going to accept.'

They said, 'Very funny, young man. You need to apply. The Plessy Radar vacancy has got 300 applicants and Ford Motor Company over 400.' I said 'Okay, I'll be back in a few weeks once I've got in and I'll tell you which one I want to take.' I could see in their faces they thought "Cheeky rascal!"

I genuinely believed that I would go and be interviewed and I would tell the companies whether I was going to accept them or not. 'You think you can or you think you can't, you're probably right.' Anyway, three weeks later I'd been offered the sponsorship by both companies and I went with Ford. I hope this doesn't sound too arrogant, I was just absolutely clear that nothing was going to stop me getting the sponsorship money. It was more important than anything else to me at that time. The reason I got offered the opportunity was simple: It was more important to me than any one of those other 700 young people.

In my very first term at North East London Polytechnic (NELP) I can remember I got a grant check of £400. Then Mrs Thatcher axed grants for almost all students and in my second term I got a grant check for £1.50 and in my third term I got nothing at all. The Ford sponsorship meant a lot to me. It was incredibly generous, and I've got a tear of gratitude in my eye for Ford as I tell you this. My sponsorship was a huge £1,000 per term. I did two terms at NELP for four years and then for each of the other six months I would go and work for Ford.

It wasn't easy work, it was hard shift work. It was twelve hour days and twelve hour nights and of the thirty students that started at Ford in my year, not all studying at NELP but spread all around the UK, only three of us actually made it to the other end of the programme and graduated.

Going to NELP as a sponsored student allowed my first steps in property. Why? Because I wanted to buy a property . I had my Mum's £250 and I was determined not to waste it like many students would.

My contemporaries, many of them from more affluent backgrounds than me, seemed to just drink whatever money their parents gave them. Then they'd say, 'Oh, Mum and Dad, I've run out of money, could you send me some more?' And their parents did! I remember one of them, the poshest kid in the class, his parents gave him a car for his eighteenth birthday. He wrote it off, and said 'oh, Mum and Dad I've broken my car,' and they gave him another one! I remember thinking what kind of lunatic would do that? I just thought it was totally disrespectful.

I'd fixed one half of my problem now. I was getting paid to go to NELP and in my first two terms I received the £2,000 from Fords. In my very first term I also got £400 as a grant before Mrs Thatcher stopped most students receiving grants. Then, in the six months of that year that I was actually working for Fords, this was as an eighteen-year-old in 1982, I managed to earn another £8,000. That was a lot of money back then. In my first year as a student I earned more than £10,000.

I checked the Office for National Statistics website and in 1982 average pay was just under £10,000 per year. As a student working for just 6 months of the year I was already earning the national average income.

I was doing factory work, I was doing twelve hour day shifts and twelve hour night shifts. I worked a week of days followed by a week of nights. I saw some things that an eighteen-year-old probably shouldn't have seen, but I made a decent amount of money.

So now to the second part of my conundrum, how could I live for virtually nothing? I don't know if you've ever asked yourself that question. I was scouring all the local papers and talking to the local agents and I ended up finding an advert in the local paper. In essence it said, 'Free accommodation, call this number.' So, I phoned the number, I mean what was the worst that could happen? I appreciate that perhaps a slightly more timid or younger person might not have gone for it, it did feel a bit strange, but I was driven by my goal to live for virtually nothing.

I phoned the number, a man answered, after introducing myself I said, 'I've seen your advert in the paper, free accommodation. What do you want in exchange?'. I often hear people say "If it seems too good to be true it probably is" or "No such thing as a free lunch" and I am pretty sure most people would not have called the number as they would have believed such "wisdom". What if, just what if it was true and I had not made a simple phone call?

Here was the deal, It was the servant's accommodation in a country manor house just off the M25 near Cheshunt. What I had to give in exchange was twenty hours work per week. This included gardening, sweeping the tennis courts, sorting out the swimming pool and many other similar tasks. It was a gorgeous house. I got a two bedroom flat completely for free, all bills included, in exchange for work. All I had to pay for was my food and transport. They were a very kind family and I really enjoyed my time there. This experience also helped me, a working class kid from a pit village, that normal people can live in very nice houses. The family were builders. More evidence that property pays handsomely. I decided one day I would own a big house in the country with grounds.

I set myself a budget for food and travel of £10 a week. This now meant I was earning in excess of £10,000 a year and my living costs were just £10 a week.

The few people I have previously told about my £10,000 a year with £10 a week living costs have typically had this reaction: "You are so lucky". Really? I don't think I was lucky, I think I was prepared to do things that others would not and soon I was able to do things that others could not. I would encourage everyone to ask high quality questions and act with clarity and purpose. I repeat what I said earlier:

'The quality of the questions you ask determines the quality of answers you get, and in turn that determines the quality of your life.'

Now I decided to spend Mum's money, because that's how I thought of it, Mum's money. I know Dad contributed too, so I don't know if it was Dad's wages or Mum's Tupperware money. I invested Mum's money in a motorbike. Why? The Manor House where I was living was about twenty miles away from NELP and about thirty miles from Ford in Dagenham. This allowed me to achieve my budget of £10 per week for food and transport.

As a first year student I got myself a sponsorship, was being educated at NELP and I was being educated in a factory. Full time, £10,000 income, virtually no living expenses and £10 covered my groceries and my petrol. I didn't really do much else I had no time. Studying or working shifts plus 20 hours work a week at the Manor House. I'm not saying I never socialised or had a beer, I would go to the student's union, and back then we were talking pennies per pint. I would only do that if I had any spare money from my £10. Jim Rohn said "Discipline is the bridge between goals and accomplishment". My simple routine disciplines were my bridge between my goals of not costing my parents anything, getting a degree and buying a property all at the same time.

I had a fantastic life. I was living in a country manor for free! The family I worked for were very generous and friendly. When they went travelling, as they often did, they would let my friends come around and we could use the tennis courts and the swimming pool. They even let me have a party in the pool house one time. Life was absolutely fabulous. If I hadn't asked myself the questions, 'how can I get paid to go to university', and 'how can I live for nothing?' I wouldn't have got the answers I wanted. I don't accept that it was any easier or harder for me to ask that question then than it would be for a student now. If you want a better quality of answer, ask a better quality of question.

What did this mean financially for me? It meant that my bank account was filling up with money pretty quickly. A year into university and working for Fords I had a serious amount stashed away. I had bought my motorbike for £175, insured it and spent my £10 a week for my petrol and my food. The only significant expense I had was income tax. The sponsorship and grant money were tax free, I had a £1,565 personal tax allowance and after that I paid 30% income tax on my Ford earnings. My total tax and national insurance in that first 12 months was £2,205 and £520 for a years food and petrol.

Income £10,000 expenses £2,205 tax and £520 living expenses left me with £7,275 in the bank. The bank could see that I was serious about operating my finances properly, so they gave me a credit card and an overdraft facility.

Before I went back for my second year at university I thanked the family at the Manor House that I'd been living with. They were very nice people and they seemed happy with me because I would never watch the clock and would often do extra hours. I can remember one Saturday afternoon I got myself badly sun burned. They had a one acre rose garden in one part of the grounds. I was pruning this rose garden for about eight hours, it was very relaxing and my mind was coming up with great ideas. The time was flying by. It was blazing sunshine and I burned badly. The family saw me 'What have you done? You're like a lobster!' Then I had bright red hair and many freckles, I've never gone brown in the sunshine in my life. I eventually go dark red like a Native American. So, I came in that day looking like a Cherokee crossed with a lobster.

I feel blessed in many ways. Over the years I have always challenged myself to ask a good quality of question. We are now at the end of my "First Steps". At this point I have built up a "war chest" of £7,275. I had managed to do this while studying at NELP, having virtually no expenses and earning a very decent amount of income. See you in chapter four where we're going to go from First Steps to First Property. I hope you are enjoying the book so far.

Chapter Four: First Property

Shopping time! I've shared my early influences, first refurbishment, my understandings and my first lessons, my mentors, my father, my mother and my grandfathers on both sides. I shared with you, with a tear in my eye, when my mother gave me that money that I wasn't expecting and the determination that it gave me to never waste it.

At that stage, I wasn't very financially sophisticated. I didn't yet understand things like mortgages. I didn't really know what property cost. All I knew was I had £7,275 and it was time to go shopping!

I started looking around East Ham in London. I had simply put a pin in the map. Logistically, it was halfway between the two places I needed to get myself to, NELP for studying and Dagenham for working at Fords. Property buying was a new world to me.

It took me about six estate agents before one of them didn't just laugh at me and kick me out the front door. They thought I was some sort of bum. I must have been quite a sight: Six-foot-tall, copper red hair that came down over my shoulders and I used to wear leather all the time as a motorcyclist to protect myself if I came off. You can imagine it, can't you? This fresh faced eighteen-year-old, long red hair and a motorbike jacket turns up on his motorbike, parks it outside the estate agent, goes in and asks 'What properties have you got that would suit me?'

In case you are wondering why not use Rightmove on the internet this was 1982, it did not exist!

"Never judge a book by its cover" is one of my maxims. A friend of mine, for example his net-worth is way in excess of £500m, if you saw him I the street he will be wearing his £10 Costco trainers. You know, the Kirkland brand Costco trainers and a coat that looks like his Granddad left it to him fifty years ago. You would never know that he is such a wealthy man.

Appearance and nice clothes, they're just not important to him.

So, I got judged and I had to learn not to react when I was judged. I was often judged for instance by the police. It wouldn't happen these days, it would probably be illegal. On a weekly basis, if not more than that, I was stopped and searched by the police. One time I can remember that the policeman stopped me in East Ham. I was perceived to be a "biker" and I guess I was. That was the lifestyle that I chose and that was the way I chose to appear to the outside world, the persona I adopted. This policeman said, 'Look, let's just do this the easy way. Tell me where the drugs are and when we get it over with, if you don't have a record I'll just give you a warning.' I said, 'I don't have any drugs.' He used a rude word and said, essentially, 'don't be ridiculous.' Then he proceeded to almost strip-search me there in the street. I had my jacket off, I had my jumper off, I had my t-shirt off. He was poking around in my pockets and I'm stood there in a pair of jeans in the middle of the street with this policeman doing what he thought he needed to do.

He couldn't find anything and as I was getting dressed again he saw that the bike had one of those big lock boxes on the back. He said, 'What's in the box?' I said, 'Books.' He said, 'What do you mean, books?' I said, 'Well, I need quite a lot of books for my studies.' 'You don't go to university,' I assured him that I did. 'I don't believe you,' he replied. 'Well, whether you believe me or not, it's not really material, is it? I know what I do, you don't. You asked me a question, I told you the answer.'

He perceived this to be impertinance, although I was purposefully being extremely neutral and calm and just answering his questions. It was almost like the calmer I was the more aggravated he was getting and so he used more rude words. He said, 'Open the box.' I said, 'I'm not sure I have to.' He said, 'Oh, right. Smart-arse are you?' I said, 'I will open the box. I'm not sure I have to, and I think, officer, when we've completed this conversation, I'll be wanting to take a note of your number and I'll be having conversations as to whether I should take this further.' 'Oh, threatening me now, are we?

Open this f-ing box now.' So, I opened the box and in it were books, just as I had said, and under the books was a chain and padlock.

He said, 'This is a concealed weapon.' Again I stayed calm 'No, it's not. It's a chain and a padlock to lock up my motorbike.' He was not convinced 'I'm confiscating this. This is a concealed weapon.' I needed my chain and padlock as East London was not the place to be leaving a motorbike unlocked.. 'I'm not going to challenge your authority officer, I'm just going to do something about it.' He said, 'What do you mean?' I said, 'There are always choices, officer, and there are always consequences.' And he said, 'Are you threatening me?' I assured him I was not 'No, not at all. But you are taking away from me one of my possessions, which I have perfectly legitimately. You show me a motorcyclist that doesn't have a chain to secure his motorbike. Show me one.' He repeated, 'It's a concealed weapon.' In resignation I replied 'All right officer, I might not be as up to speed with all the ins and outs of it as far as concealed weapons are concerned, but I thought to be a concealed weapon it had to be on my body. You should know better than me.'

I was just about to putting my jacket back on and he said, 'Give me that jacket.' So I gave him my jacket and he pulled out what I can only describe as a flick-knife and he started shredding the lining of my jacket. I was appalled, 'What are you doing?' He said, 'I've just worked out where your drugs are. I saw something when you were just about to put that jacket back on. There's something in there.' I was now confused 'News to me if there is, but what's the compensation procedure for you shredding the lining of my jacket?' And he said, 'I haven't shredded the lining of your jacket. It was like this when you gave it to me. You can't prove it wasn't.'

There was indeed something inside the lining of my jacket. The jacket was quite worn. I'd had a pen that I loved, that my English Granddad had given to me and I'd lost it. I'd been wearing the jacket for so long that a hole had appeared in the lining inside one of the pockets and the pen had gone down inside it. So, I didn't know, but I had a ballpoint pen inside the lining of my jacket. He threw my jacket back at me. He threw the pen at me. I was delighted to find the pen so I started smiling. I used the pen, this is ironic isn't it, I used the pen to write the PC's number on my hand. He was subject to disciplinary proceedings shortly afterwards. He initially denied everything but I had spent time collecting a number of witnesses at the scene. The vast majority of people are very kind and decent. They did not like what he had done to me. It could have ended so differently if I'd reacted differently.

One of my favourite Mark Twain quotes is: "Never argue with stupid people. They will pull you down to their level and then beat you with experience."

The reason I went off into the policeman story is to share that I was used to being judged and the agents were judging me the same way. I had money to spend, but they assumed that I didn't. It took me a while to get an agent that took me seriously. When I did, I viewed just five properties and I ended up buying 269 Roman Road, East Ham. It was a house that had been converted into an upper flat and a lower flat. I bought the upper flat. It came with a garden and it had a garage. It was delighted with my one bedroom flat.

This would be at the end of 1983. I was eighteen years old, nineteen later that year, and I had bought my first flat. 269 Roman Road, East Ham. The price was almost, but not quite, £11,000. I had £7,275 in cash. I went to see my bank manager (we still had them then). After helpful discussions about legal costs and making allowances for furnishing plus cooker, fridge, washing machine and all the other things I would need I agreed a loan with him of £4,500 and bought my first property.

Even at just eighteen years old I was totally confident it was the right thing for me to do. None of my friends had a clue what I was doing. None of them knew I was working so hard. None of them knew why I wasn't partying hard. I now had an £11,000 flat whilst they were living in student digs, paying for the privilege and not earning any money. So that was my first property, not yet my first investment property but I was on the "property ladder".

What I want to talk about in the next chapter, chapter five, is growing my property wealth, the next five years of my property investment career, all in residential property, all in my own homes. I didn't get my first pure investment property until I was twenty-three. I really like this Warren Buffet quote "I made my first investment at eleven years old, until then I just wasted my life..." so not quite Warren Buffet but not bad!

Chapter Five: Wealth Genesis

Eighteen years of age. Now owning a flat in London, 269 Roman Road, East Ham. Earning good money. What would the next few years hold?

On average, property prices double every eight to ten years and have done, pretty consistently, since 1086. That's when the Doomsday Book was written. (Not to be confused with 1066, that was the Battle of Hastings....) I find it fascinating that the value of all the land and buildings, and all the other assets in the Doomsday Book, were valued at almost exactly £1,000,000. That was in 1086.

Roll the clock forward, not even 1,000 years to today. That might sound like a strange contrast frame to some people, not even 1,000 years. I am probably not still around if you're reading this after the year 2086 but I hope you are enjoy it!

The house that I live in now, my home on the west coast of Scotland, is valued at more than everything in the Doomsday Book. My house is worth more than the UK was not even 1,000 years ago.

That is how fast property values have appreciated over the last 900 plus years. Sometimes years there are spectacular increases in house prices and occasionally spectacular drops. You've got to be ready for both. There are different techniques to use, depending on the macro economic environment.

Now, I'm not going to pretend that at the age of eighteen I had all that sussed. Muhammad Ali once said, 'If a man's view of the world is the same at fifty, as it was at twenty, he's wasted thirty years.' I'm in my fifties now. I wasn't even twenty then. Those are wise words from Muhammad Ali. As you grow, as you mature, as you learn, your perspective changes. Your capability to add value changes. How you can help others, changes.

At eighteen I knew I didn't want to, as I a saw it, 'waste' money on renting property. I wanted to buy property. I was clear about that. I was surprised, amazed, grateful at quite how fast property prices were going up. By the age of twenty, around two years after I had purchased 269 Roman Road, I sold it. In that two years the property price had almost tripled. I sold it for £32,000. An incredible value increase. Some years my houses earned more than I did as a salary.

What did I do with my money? By that time, I was unencumbered, I had paid off the loan on that property. Selling it for £32,000 meant I had £32,000 in cash, at the age of twenty. I moved out further into Essex. I bought a two-bedroom detached house in a village called Aveley. I absolutely loved my new home.

I kept £6,000 of the profit from selling my flat. One of the perks of working for Ford at that time was that I was allowed to purchase two cars each year and get a twenty-five per cent discount. I ordered myself a brand new black XR2 with red trim. I bought that with cash, literally. I took money out of the bank, wandered up to Dagenham Motors and said "I'll have one of those, please."

Many other people at Ford did the same. We had to keep our cars for at least nine months before we could sell it them. This also moved my wealth in the right direction. I would buy a new car every nine or ten months and sell my old one, this was in the days when registration plates used to change every year, not every six months. I could sell it on a brand new registration plate for more than I paid for it. For a few years I was making money on cars. Nothing complicated or fancy, just like everybody else did at Ford. My lesson here is that a number of jobs help you make money in specialised areas. What does your current role allow you to do to make a little extra money? I learned from my environment and copied my mentors. So effectively I got a free car. A free, new car, simply by holding back some of the profits that I'd made from my first property.

That left me, after I paid my fees with around £25,000 to put down. I bought my new two-bedroom detached home for £36,000. I traded location, London, for a cheaper place, Essex. I got a much bigger property for just a few thousand pounds more and I got a free car, actually better than free as I made money on it every year.

I now had an £11,000 mortgage. I was beginning to learn about gearing and the choices that you make and the impact that has on your residual income. In another few years my income more than doubled. Once I graduated I moved out of the trainee grades. I was a foreman by this time, a production foreman. My uniform was a green lab coat with a red collar. The quality control foreman wore a green lab coat with a blue collar. The maintenance foreman had a brown collar. Both the blue and the brown collars got paid more than us. It used to amuse me to hear news articles about "white collar" or "blue collar" workers, it meant something very different to me.

When I finished college my annual work time went from six months a year to twelve months a year. It had been two terms at college then six months at Ford. This really was a "double whammy". Double the hourly rate and double the working time. A tiny mortgage and a brand new car that made me even more money plus a house that was rocketing in value. Financially this was a very happy time.

I love all our children. I have six wonderful children and a granddaughter. There was no pitter-patter of little feet at this particular point in my life. That was very, very shortly to come. While I was in that two-bedroom house in Aveley my disposable income was gigantic. It was enormous. I did things like "save up" for two months and put a conservatory on the house, paid for in cash. Another month I took my surplus income and re-carpeted the whole house. I got it all re-decorated and bought a new suite of furniture, plus a new TV.

Dire Straits released Money for Nothing in 1985. I really did feel Mark

Knopfler was talking to me through that record. If you have never listened to it get yourself a copy of Dire Straits, Money for Nothing. That is exactly how my life felt at that time.

This wasn't financial freedom because I still had to go work for my money, but what a massive income I had and what tiny outgoings.

We discovered that our oldest daughter, Becci, who is now a mother herself, was on the way. This was fabulous news! We decided to get a bigger property. The house that we had bought for £36,000 a couple of years previously quickly sold again. We got £45,000 for it.

In both cases, my first flat and our first house I could have released equity and retained the property. The flat is currently worth over £360,000 and the house around £310,000. By selling just these two properties I have so far cost myself in excess of £600,000. I did not know then what I know now and only for very specific reasons do I ever sell any property now. Property value increase over time builds huge wealth.

Ok so £45,000 sale price and roughly a £10,000 mortgage outstanding. This gave us a £35,000 deposit on our next property. We went and bought a detached three-bedroom bungalow in Aveley. It sat on over an acre of land and it had a stream a gorgeous pond and an orchard. All of this we got for £78,000.

We increased our mortgage. I had £35,000 to put down and I was buying it for £78,000 so my mortgage was £32,000. At the time, there was a tax break that doesn't exist anymore. We used to be able to claim tax relief against our income tax on the first £30,000 per person for a residential mortgage. This was called MIRAS, mortgage interest relief at source. It was a great tax break and really helped with the mortgage payments.

Over time, the tax breaks change. The way the government taxes you changes over the decades. Here's the key thing; as long as you keep up to speed with that, as long as you have knowledge of what is and isn't allowed, as long as you continually invest in your education, you can not only save a fortune, you can earn a fortune and create wealth.

I was twenty-two years old, I was buying a three-bedroom bungalow on over an acre of land and preparing for my first child to arrive. When I tell people this they find it hard to believe. They make statements like "You were so lucky. But of course, you couldn't do that now....". Really? Was I lucky or disciplined? As for "you couldn't do that now" well Becci and Jack, our oldest son, both have their own homes. Jack bought his first flat at eighteen, just like I did. He has investment property too, his is Serviced Accommodation.

Once more "If you think you can, or you think you can't you are probably right...". In a general sense the only person that's ever going to stop you doing anything, is you. As long as you get past that, as long as you, to use that Americanism, 'get over yourself', you are going to be able to achieve anything you set your heart on.

I was now in a £78,000 property and my property value was now just a touch over seven times the value my first flat in East Ham. My equity, my cash if I wanted to sell my bungalow, had gone from £7,275 to £36,000 and I had taken £6,000 to buy a new car from my flat sale as well. You may be familiar with this expression: "a rising tide floats all boats." When the property market is in boom as it was then you need all of your cash invested to make sure that you're gathering up as much possible benefit from the increase in prices as you can but you don't want to over-gear. In other words to borrow what you cannot afford to repay.

Let's take a closer look at the impact of property price rises. My first flat was an £11,000 property. When it goes up by ten per cent, that's £1,100. My £78,000 bungalow also goes up by ten per cent, well that's £7,800. Is all that £78,000 mine? No. Only half of it was, the other half was borrowed. So, a ten per cent increase (which I keep all of it), where fifty per cent wasn't even my money. I'm getting a huge return on money that's not mine. I can't really see a problem with that, as long as you're not over-geared and putting your assets in danger. The thing you have to watch out for is property prices dropping and interest rates going up. We'll come back to more of that later in this book.

By the end of this five year period finished, I'd been in my flat a couple of years, I'd been in my little house for just over two years, and I'd been in my bungalow forty-two weeks.

I worked for Ford as a sponsored under-graduate and then I worked for Ford after graduating. I received a job offer to go North and work for Rowntree's as a production manager, this was a senior management position. This would mean leaving the factory floor and to stop being paid hourly, with overtime and doing shifts with shift pay. I would change from hourly pay to salary. My basic pay (salary) was higher but my take-home would go down a lot because I wouldn't get any shift work premium and I wouldn't get any overtime pay.

In the next chapter, I'm going to address how I balanced the financial risk and the decision I took to go North to develop my career and to take a step up into senior management at the age of twenty-three. I went to work for Rowntree Mackintosh. The company was purchased by Nestle whilst I was there. I was working in Newcastle in an area called Fawdon. My title was "Chocolate Production Manager" and 300 people were working for me. I was responsible for manufacturing the Toffee Crisp and Lion bar. It was like "Charlie and the Chocolate Factory". I loved this job.

I don't talk very often about this period in my career because it's so short, just a year and a half, but some hugely important lessons came to me during this period. Property then was "the gift that keeps on giving", the fabulous bungalow that we bought we owned for forty-two weeks. How do I remember so clearly years later that is was 42 weeks? Well, we purchased it for £78,000 and sold it forty-two weeks later for £120,000.

That bungalow earned us £1,000 a week, between the ages of twenty-two and twenty-three. Far more than I was earning in my job and all of it completely tax free, because it was appreciation on my PPR, my Principal Private Residence. Our home. No capital gains tax and no income tax on your home when it increases in value.

The government is capable of all sorts of things, but to change the rules on capital gains tax for our homes, even for our fabulous government, would just be one massive step too far. They'd have civil war, they'd have riots if they did that. They'd certainly get voted out.

Let's just recap on the boom times, the happy times, the golden times. I bought a flat, for £11,000, when I was eighteen. By the time I was twenty-three we had sold a bungalow for £120,000, with a £35,000 mortgage on it. How much cash did we have? We had £85,000 having started off with £7,275 just 5 years earlier.

What strategy gained that wealth for us? Property. Not forgetting that I also pulled out £6,000 which I put into my black XR2. I'm going to add back in the £500 a year that I made from buying and selling the cars. It wasn't a fortune, but that was typically how much I would earn over and above the price of my new car. For five years and that is another £2,500 on top of the £6,000 I pulled out. That's another £8,500. The latest car was on my drive all paid for.

Add the £8,500 car to my £85,000 in cash is a total of £93,500 all from an initial £7,275 investment. Five years on and I had multiplied my wealth by a staggering 1,285%.

What are the lessons I draw from this phase in my life?

First the single most expensive mistake you can make in property is not to have any. I didn't make that mistake. Here is one of my quotes:

"Buy houses and wait, don't wait to buy houses!"

Second in the good times you need to get as much capital as you can afford deployed. A £100,000 house going up by ten per cent gives you £10,000 but a £1,000,000 portfolio going up by ten per cent gives you £100,000. Here is my quote on using other the banks money (mortgages) and enjoying property value increases:

"Infinity is not a theoretical concept. Controlled Property Investment makes it a reality."

We need education, we need support, we all need mentoring. We all need to know what we're doing. For anybody who thinks education's expensive, trust me, ignorance is far, far more expensive. Just imagine if I had not invested in my first flat because it "seemed too good to be true."

Third never sell good property. Did I have the salary so that rather than sell my first flat I could have raised money against it and reinvested that back? Released equity and reinvested that in more properties? In other words, could I have bought my two-bedroom house in Aveley and kept my flat in East London and rented it out? As well as my flat in East London, could I have kept my two-bedroom house in Aveley and rented it out? I could have, if I'd known what I was doing, but that would have been one hell of a big ask, a huge ask, and I'll explain why. I could have done it, but I didn't know how to. As before "If you think education is expensive try ignorance." On the very conservative side, ignoring rental profits if I still had my first flat, house and bungalow I would have a minimum of an extra £1,000,000 in equity and probably a lot more.

Perhaps if there had there been an educational course that I could have gone to I would have done. I'm talking about the 1980s and this isn't something that "normal" people did. Yes, there were professional landlords, but that was a closed clique. It was not something that I knew anything about. Not something I had any connections to. That all changed in 1996, a decade after I was doing all this. What happened in 1996? It became possible to get buy-to-let mortgages. Prior to that? Impossible. They didn't exist.

So, why is this third point a massively powerful lesson? Think how much more compound wealth I could have had in my family's legacy, if I'd had known a few basic facts.

Which is why I say, and I say unapologetically, for all those out there that say that "education's expensive", I say "try ignorance, that's really expensive". Even if I'd spent £30,000 on a course, which I couldn't because there weren't any in the 1980's, and if the only thing the course taught me was "don't sell property" just from my first three properties I would be over £1,000,000 better off today. When you hear me speak you will hear me say:

"If you think education is expensive, try ignorance...."

The next biggest mistake to not investing in property is not investing in yourself. Jim Rohn said: 'school education will earn you a living, self-education will earn you a fortune.' I think that is so true. For many years, since the early 2000's, I've been strongly invested in myself. If I go on a course and I just learn one little thing, one nugget, I don't care what I pay for the course. I will recover the cost time and time and time again.

These are my lessons from that five years. I look forward to seeing you in the next chapter, which is working the North, investing in the South, my first investment property.

Chapter Six: My First Hard Lesson

The first of "Six of the Best". Welcome to 1987. To remind you, or if you've just jumped in to read this chapter, I've just been offered a promotion, I have sold my bungalow in Essex and I am moving to Newcastle. I'm going to be the production manager for Toffee Crisp and Lion Bar at Rowntree's. That in itself is a whole book that I look forward to writing one day. So many memories, so many learnings, so much support, so much challenge.

Moving so far away with a young child and no family around us would bring a whole new set of challenges. I thought I was going to be working at Rowntree's for a long time but it wasn't to be.

I had just enjoyed five years of huge capital growth in the South East. I had researched property prices in the North East and prices had barely moved over the same five years.

So, here's what I did. I decided to take some of our money and buy a house just outside Newcastle. At the same time I decided to use some of our money for a deposit on a much larger detached house in Aveley. The house in Aveley was a joint venture with – this is before I even knew what a joint venture was – my best friend.

I'd got the idea of having a rental property by then and even though this was before buy-to-let mortgages, I did what some people did at that time, I bought a house with a friend. Back then you could get up to four people on the mortgage. Why? Well, do you remember the £30,000 MIRAS tax relief you could set against your mortgage from your PAYE income? Well you could have up to four people claiming on the same property. My behaviour was partially driven by the tax legislation situation at that time and partly driven by the fact that I still wanted to be exposed to the South East property market but I didn't want to be managing a property 300 miles from where I was going to be living. Importantly it was also driven by friendship.

The solution that was agreed was we would take some of our money and buy a family home. At the time, it was my previous wife, my daughter, Becci, and me so we didn't need a big house, just the three of us. We would also buy a house in the South East with my friend Nick. We bought a three-bedroom detached house in Aveley. It was a really nice, modern three-bedroom detached house.

This was a balanced approach: Spread the money and minimise risk with a joint venture. What could possibly go wrong? Well, let's take one element at a time and analyse more deeply what was going on.

Element One:

My first task was to negotiate my release from the Ford Motor Company. I wasn't working at the Dagenham plant by now, instead I was south of the river Thames at the Woolwich component plant and they had announced the closure of the site. I was a foreman and I was in the union, believe it or not. I was junior management but all of us were in the union. My trade union, who were very strong at this time, because of the plant closure helped me a lot.

Even though the company knew I was leaving, I was still able to claim redundancy. The union had an incredible redundancy package negotiated, I got two years pay. My basic pay then was £12,000 pounds, so I got £24,000 pounds tax free. The company had to pay this even though they knew I had another job, how crazy is that? Thank you very much! Once the three-bed bungalow in Aveley sold I had £109,000 in cash, all tax paid.

This was not an accident. I knew I could get redundancy as the plant was closing. Ford wanted to move me back to Dagenham, I wanted to develop my career fast. That meant moving companies a few times. The statistics are clear: you will gain promotion far faster if you are prepared to move companies to achieve this.

In order to take advantage of an opportunity first we have to recognise it. Many of my colleagues at the time valued "job security" over redundancy. I was clear my best career option was to get a promotion and take the tax free redundancy.

We all feel fear, this is an emotional reaction. Courage is a decision despite any fear we may feel. To achieve wealth we cannot do what average people do, that leads to average results.

Element Two

When you diversify and "don't have all of your eggs in one basket", rather you have multiple strategies, multiple different ways of earning income and then you're far less likely to be disrupted by any one single event. This proved sound.

The next part of the plan was buying our family home. We bought a relatively modern, three story, three-bedroom townhouse in a lovely village called Wylam. This was just off, what the locals call, the 'military road' the A69. It was about a twenty minute journey on my motorbike to work. We chose Wylam for a couple of different reasons.

Reason one was that we were moving away from any close family support. Living in Wylam gave us some family support because my then brother-in-law, Jeremy, had married a girl from Wylam and her family all lived there. They were lovely people and they gave us a lot of help. Any young family with a little baby needs all the help they can get.

My second reason was that Wylam was a gorgeous place and I enjoyed the twenty minute commute into work. It allowed me to get my head straight and let me think. I used to love riding the bike on those open roads. It was a nice lifestyle.

When you move to a new area or a new place you don't always decide where you're going to live straight away. To make sure we were moving the right area and that we got the right house I moved up a few months ahead of the family and I stayed with two of my relatives-in-law. They were a lovely couple and they were very kind to me. I paid them a very modest board and lodging and that allowed me to do the local property research. We decided to move to Wylam and we paid £36,000 pounds for a spacious three-bed town house over three floors with a garage and some storage space on the ground floor. The lounge, dining room and kitchen were on the first floor and all the bedrooms were on the second floor, a traditional town house construction.

The house in Aveley, which is the main lesson in this chapter I will return to later, cost £125,000. I also kept £20,000 in cash because I had decided to diversify out of property and into other asset classes. I wasn't quite sure what I was going to invest it in, I just wanted a war chest.

We had a £109,000 cash. I was buying a £125,000 investment property and our £36,000 home, total property value £161,000. I wanted to keep £20,000 in cash. Between the two houses I could put down £89,000 of deposits. To get two mortgages for a combined total of £62,000 wasn't hard, I was borrowing less than half the property values. My new basic salary in my role as production manager at Rowntree's at that time was £16,5000 which was fine for £62,000 of mortgages.

Element Three

Diversifying from property. While I was at Rowntree's the company was taken over by Nestle, who still own it. Within a week of my arrival there was takeover frenzy. I had made a conscious decision that I wanted to invest in a different asset class other than property. The share price when I arrived was £3.60 and the entire company was talking about it, I'm not even going to say on an hourly basis, they were talking about it on a minute by minute basis. It wasn't "insider knowledge", it was all in the public domain but because we were staff, we were getting briefed by the directors on an almost daily basis about what was happening with the takeover. I hosted my first VIP visit during the take-over. I was the senior manager on the site as my General Manager had gone on holiday. Neil Kinnock, then the Labour Party leader, announced that he was going to support the campaign to keep Rowntree Mackintosh British and not allow it to be taken over by Nestle, obviously an international company, so he came and visited the factory.

Many times, politicians try and do the right thing, hopefully for the right reasons, but ultimately in this particular case Neil Kinnock, along with the other efforts to keep Nestle at bay, failed. During that period, I took the decision to invest in Rowntree shares. I felt informed, I was very close to the action and I had the cash. I wanted to have other interests besides property, so this seemed like the ideal opportunity. From my £20,000 cash war chest I invested £10,000.

Within six months the takeover had happened and the shares had gone from £3.60 all the way up to £10.80. I tripled my money in six months. I kept £10,000 in cash and I invested £10,000 in shares, within six months, my shares were worth £30,000 pounds.

I'm not claiming I'm an expert stock picker, I'm far from being the next Warren Buffet. Shares are not my main strategy but it's just interesting that if it hadn't been for property, I couldn't have done that because I wouldn't have had the cash. So, the £20,000 worth of profit from shres, was it directly from property? No. Was it enabled by property? One hundred per cent, all the way.

To finish the story on the three-bedroom townhouse in Wylam, we owned that for a year and a half before we moved back to the South East again for another promotion. We sold that £36,000 townhouse for £52,000. So actually, with the benefit of hindsight, I could have taken all my money to the North East and I would have had an even larger gain.

In general when London or the South prices slow or flatten out then prices in the regions rise. This was one of those moments in time. I hadn't seen this cycle before, I hadn't got enough experience, I didn't have a mentor telling me this would happen. I did okay overall, with an experienced mentor I may well have done better.

We made money on our home in Wylam, we made more money from our Rowntree shares. We made many good friends. Together with experiences like going out on a Saturday night in the "Big Market" and learning to windsurf on the lakes of Northumberland I really enjoyed my time there.

Element Four

I want to concentrate for the rest of this chapter on what happened to my three-bed investment in Essex.

Surely, if my property in Newcastle had gone from £36,000 to £52,000 the one in Essex had gone from £125,000 to a lot more than that, right? Well, you'd have thought so, wouldn't you? It didn't turn out that way.

For every boom there's a bust and this was a strong down-turn in the South East. I was twenty-four years old by now it was 1989 almost 1990. In the early 1990's London and the South East property market "caught a cold". A bad cold. I had invested £125,000 with Nick in Aveley and I'm going to talk in more detail about what I learned, what I could have done better, how it changed my approach and how it stopped me investing in property for far too long.

Why is this the first of my Six of The Best? This house taught me a real lesson. I'm sure you've heard this said before:

"Either you earn, or you learn."

Well, I've certainly learned on this property.

We bought three quarters of the house in Aveley and my good friend Nick bought a quarter of the house. All very equitable, all very friendly. He would then live in the house and we would spend the odd weekend doing it up together, not that it really needed much doing, it was in pretty good condition. Nick would then take in lodgers for me. Two in the other bedrooms and one in the lounge. So in theory, he gets to live there and he's got a quarter of the house, so he's enjoying a quarter of an asset. I'd got three lodgers bringing in three lots of room rental income.

Nick as part of the bargain, in return for living where he was living, was to be, the property manager, looking after three quarters of the house and living in the other quarter. He was working in London at the time and the commute was OK to London by train. The rent that came in should obviously be more than enough to pay my mortgage and the rest of the money would be profit for me. For Nick, it wasn't an income-generating asset, it was his home. The plan was we would share the capital growth that we both expected.

Nick was my best friend then and he still is now, more than thirty years later.

So, what had we just done? We had just completed a joint venture, although if you'd asked either of us, 'is this a joint venture?' we'd have probably given you a sideways look as we wouldn't really have known what you were talking about. It was literally a joint venture. He lived in it and benefited from that. For me, it was an investment vehicle. I didn't want to live in it, I wanted to keep my money working, because as you have seen I'd gone from less than £10,000 to more than £90,000 in just five years.

We felt property in the South East couldn't lose. I felt was going to be great because I was going to be earning good money in my new job and, over above that, I had another house that might also make me some money. I didn't think it was very likely at the time but in theory it could. I'd done this amazing deal with Ford to gain more wealth by taking redundancy, and I'd learned for the first time how to invest very profitably with stocks and shares.

My venture with Nick was to be the pièce de résistance. That was my plan.

Very quickly I did the deal with Nick, we just shook hands. The paperwork followed and accurately reflected our deal. There was never any problem with that. I owned three quarters of the house and Nick owned one quarter of the house. It was documented that I would get my deposit money back first before we divided up any profits. Nick moved in and very quickly we got the house ready for lodgers. A bit of painting, a bit of decoration some minor repairs. It took just two weekends, a few tins of paint, the odd trip to B&Q and it was sorted. We were ready for business.

What had we done? We'd done a joint venture on an HMO, a "House in Multiple Occupation". But this was in 1989. There was no such thing as an HMO. I'd never heard of an HMO and there certainly weren't any HMO regulations back then. There were no requirements for fire doors and emergency lighting or mains interlinked smoke detectors. All of those things were for the future. HMOs had yet to be invented. As far as we were concerned, we were looking for some lodgers.

This was before the Internet was commercialised. There were no sites like 'Easy Room Mate' or 'Spare Room', to simply and quickly find lodgers. We had to use adverts in the local newspapers. I didn't have time to get involved in that process because I was working full-time, I had a young family and I was 300 miles away. Nick was also working hard full-time building a career, he had a social life and recruiting lodgers so that my mortgage burden was lighter was not understandably not top of his priority list. It was a joint venture, but had we set up this joint venture correctly and fairly? You could argue fairly, I suppose, but correctly? I think not.

It was my fault. Nick had no incentive to let my rooms out. His liability was quarter of the mortgage and my liability was three quarters of the mortgage. All of the benefit of the rental income would come to me. There was literally no inducement for Nick to recruit any lodgers. In fact, you could argue that there was a disincentive because if he recruited any lodgers then suddenly he'd have to share his nice three-bedroom detached house with strangers. Suddenly, instead of being on his own doing whatever he wanted, he'd have to manage an HMO!

Over that entire eighteen-month period I had income from lodgers for just a few weeks. If I had set it up correctly, I could have expected significant lodger income from my three letting rooms. I paid three quarters of the mortgage for a property I didn't live in for a year and a half.

With hindsight, what would I have done differently? I would still have done it because the analysis I did at the time was sound. Keeping money invested in the South East and diversifying risk was sensible. Having accumulated wealth we need to learn how to preserve wealth.

It is testament to my friendship with Nick that I can say this in writing, I would have set up the joint venture differently. Of course Nick may then well not have done it at all. The way I would have proposed to revise the set up would be that Nick got a benefit from letting out the rooms, for example a percentage of the rent. He was not only paying a quarter of the mortgage, but he would have been doing all the management too. Should we have gone fifty-fifty on profit?

Perhaps I could have proposed I pay half the mortgage, even though I own three quarters of the house and Nick would pay half the mortgage. Who knows if he would have agreed, I never suggested it to him. In addition I could have said: once my mortgage is paid in its entirety by rent, we split the profit on the additional rent fifty-fifty. This would have given Nick an incentive. I wasn't thinking like that. I hadn't been trained, I didn't have a mentor. There was no part of my thinking that was shaped by providing an incentive to Nick.

We had done a joint venture on something called an HMO that hadn't been invented yet. I hadn't set it up correctly. As a result of that I reaped my just rewards: I made a huge loss on the rental income because essentially, I didn't get any. I got a just few weeks rental income but paid three quarters of the mortgage for a year and a half.

In terms of cash-flow, I was losing hundreds of pounds a month, and for the sake of an easy number to calculate let's call it £500. Interest rates were much higher in 1989/1990 than they have been from 2008 onwards. The historical average mortgage interest rate is seven per cent. There was also no such thing then as an interest only mortgage. It was a capital and interest repayment mortgage I had.

Don't get me wrong, I wasn't going bust. I could afford it, but in a way that often makes wealth erosion worse. Here's another lesson for you: the easiest way to lose money is when you've got some. If every pound is a prisoner, and every decision you make has the feeling of, 'I need to make this money work for me otherwise it's financial Armageddon,' then you will make a better quality of decision. You will ask yourself better quality questions.

So, if you have got "spare money", unless you're extraordinarily disciplined and unless you place a very high value on money and wealth, you're likely to give it away.

Wealth creators never have "spare money", those that think they do soon lose it.

With the benefit of decades of reflection, not because I regret losing the money, rather because I want to learn the lessons, "you're either earning or you're learning". What I have learned is that I was placing far too low a value on my money because I had a lot of it. I was earning a good salary, I'd done really well on my shares, my house in Wylam, was going up in value, so I didn't need the house in Essex to perform. If I had got my head around it, could I have made it perform? Absolutely.

Unless you put a very high value on money, you care for it and you nurture it, you will give it away. Look at lottery millionaires, for example. How long do they stay lottery millionaires, typically? Not very long, because they're suddenly incredibly wealthy but they're not trained to have so much money, they're not educated about money, they aren't given any mentors or support. They'll fritter it away. They'll give it to their 'friends.' They'll buy liabilities, not assets. They'll buy things that consume money, not produce money. Typically, after a year most of those millionaires are not millionaires any more. They are, broke, miserable, and often divorced. Many of them say winning the lottery was the worst thing that ever happened to them.

Now, this wasn't severe for me because financially I was still strong. I was earning in various other parts of my portfolio. I was creating wealth, but that does not excuse the fact that I lost money on a poorly performing asset. I tied up in excess of £50,000 to invest in an asset, and I use that word loosely, that didn't produce any cash-flow. 'Never mind,' I can hear you saying. 'At least you're going to benefit from the capital growth.' That's what I was thinking, let's see how that goes.... .

So, to recap, I'd completed a joint venture with my best friend on poor terms for both of us and I'd lost cash-flow.

A year and a half later and I'd got another promotion, which I'll talk about in the next chapter, in Milton Keynes. I'm twenty-five at this point and I would like my money out of the house in Aveley so that I can get the biggest home that I can afford for my family to live in. My oldest Jack is on the way, so we wanted a family home now, a big home.

Nick was fine with my request to put the house in Aveley on the market. We bought the house between us for £125,000. Add legal fees and stamp duty for the sake of a round number, let's say total costs £128,000. But at least we had the benefit of capital growth over the eighteen-month period, right?

Wrong!

The capital growth over that period was minus £10,000, so instead of putting it on the market for £125,000 the best price the local agents told us we'd get for it was £115,000. Within a few months, luckily I guess you could say, we had a buyer. That buyer was prepared to pay £115,000 and then we had to account for fees. The total purchase cost was £128,000 we sold it for £115,000. Minus 1.5% for the estate agent fees and then add legal fees making around £3,000 in total costs. The £115,000 was actually £112,000. Now the spread goes all the way from £128,000 purchase price to £112,000 net sale revenue. This resulted in a £16,000 capital loss. I had also lost money in monthly cash-flow due to my poor rental income.

'But hang on,' I hear you thinking. 'You only own three quarters of the property, Nick owns a quarter of the property. So, you've lost £12,000 and he's lost £4,000?' No. The way the agreement was written was that I got my money back first. We paid off the mortgage and all the rest of the money from the sale came to me. We were to share the profits 75%/25%. We hadn't anticipated that we could lose money and there would be no profits! He was and is my best friend. He hadn't done anything wrong. He entered into the agreement willingly with me and he agreed to sell the house to suit me, even though it must have been a pain for him.

My total losses were to the order of £26,000 including the negative monthly cash-flow on this house. That absolutely reinforced for me, without question, that property investment doesn't work. I now know this is of course not true, but I had nobody to guide me. I was in my mid-twenties and I didn't go back into property investing for almost fifteen years, not until the early 2000's. How much did that cost me? I has cost me millions if you look at what property prices did over the fifteen years I was out of the market. During this time my salary was very substantial and I could easily have added many investment properties but I didn't have anybody to tell me, 'Well actually Paul, you could've done it this way, you could've done it that way. This is what I recommend. This is how I built my property portfolio.' I didn't know anybody who was making money from investment property. I didn't have anybody in my circle of friends, I didn't have a mentor, I didn't have a mastermind.

There was no one who could say to me, 'No Paul, it's alright. Just put it in to context Paul. You've still made good money on your house in Wylam and that's more or less offset the capital loss of the house in Essex. You've made an extra twenty grand on the shares. Fantastic! Okay, you've lost ten grand in cash-flow, but if you offset that against your share money, you're still ten grand up on the whole deal and you've learned great lessons.' That's what I should have learned.

I love this quote:

"First you LEARN, then you remove the L."

Over that eighteen-month period, if you look at the whole picture, I had a capital gain in Newcastle, a capital loss in Essex, rental loss in Essex and the share price growth from Rowntree's, before it was sold to Nestle. And the sum of all that? I'd made net £10,000. Unfortunately, I wasn't focused on that. I was focused on the fact that the Essex property had cost me money.

I was completely ignoring the full story, that I started just seven years earlier with under £10,000 and I now had cash of £130,000. I was just focused on my perceived loss. There are so many lessons in here. Ultimately the most painful one was the benefit of time and the benefit of experience, because it kept me out of the investment property market for fifteen years which cost me many millions of pounds.

I'm going to go on to talk about more Six of the Best lessons in the rest of this book, the one I've just covered was the most expensive. It was the lesson that was most difficult to learn and there is only one single person to blame. As is almost always the case, the single person that stopped me learning the lessons, benefiting from the explosion in property prices over the following fifteen years when I stopped property investing, the person who hadn't taken support, education or mentoring, but had simply focused on their blue chip career; the one person responsible for all of that was me.

Let's recap on some of these lessons. When you're doing joint ventures please get some support and guidance, some wise counsel to help you make sure your joint venture is set up as a win-win. It is never about getting one over on the other person. It is never about allowing the other person to get one over on you. It is always about making sure that the joint venture is set up for the mutual benefit of all parties.

Next I was an amateur property investor who was mainly focused on his "day-job". The only education I had in the sphere of property investing was what I knew from what had worked for me in the last five years. In the context of property investing, the only strategy I understood with any depth of knowledge at all was residential property investing for a principal primary residence. I veered off into HMOs, trying to bring in lodgers and renting them a room by the week. It wasn't even an investment class that existed then. This is often referred to as "Shiny penny syndrome". Focus on what you know until you master it. Then get help to master a new strategy.

Next, it was hundreds of miles from where I lived. Bad idea....

I'd "employed" a lovely guy, a very bright guy, my best friend, as a property manager, an unpaid property manager, a disincentivised property manager and guess what? It didn't work out because it wasn't anywhere in his priorities. Nowhere. And why should it have been?

And finally, the most painful lesson to have to swallow and share with you. It convinced me that property investing didn't work. Almost anything works if you know how to do it. If you do it blindly with no knowledge and no support, almost everything doesn't work. The greatest athletes, the greatest businessmen, the greatest minds of our time, all embrace an equal measure of challenge and support. Having a mentor isn't someone that just pats you on the head and says, 'It'll be alright Paul.' No. They challenge you when they think you're doing something that's not in your best interest. They support you through the process of changing that. People who invest in themselves will create a fortune. People that accept responsibility for their actions, or lack of actions, will create a legacy.

That is the final thought that I want to leave you with in this chapter: equal measures of challenge and support, acceptance of responsibility and the importance of mentorship and a mastermind.

Onwards and upwards, "what doesn't kill you makes you stronger". I'm still here and it was a great lesson for me to learn. I'm sharing all of these lessons with you so that you learn from my mistakes. You learn through me.

Alright. Happy property investing! See you in the next chapter!

Chapter Seven: Lets Spilt! – My Second Big Lesson

It's now April 2008. Aniko, by now Mrs Smith, and me have been seriously property investing since 2003.

This property was a four-bedroom flat. We had moved to Scotland and this investment property was in the Glasgow commuter-belt town of Dumbarton. Ten minutes from Glasgow airport and ten minutes to Loch Lomond. It was a natural beauty spot and the centre of the Scottish whisky industry. There was a train into Glasgow centre every fifteen minutes and national parks nearby, so we had all sorts of things going on.

In many areas, you'll find more affordable housing sitting very close to more expensive property. For example, we now live in a village called Rhu, just outside Helensburgh. A property here would be at least twice as expensive as a similar size property in Dumbarton, despite Dumbarton being only seven miles away.

We had already made numerous investments in Dumbarton. We knew the area relatively well, it was only six or seven miles from our home and we decided to do something called a "Title Split".

Here's the basic idea. We would purchase a four-bedroomed flat and split it into two, two-bedroomed flats. Not everybody will be familiar with the Scottish property market and although it's not that different to the property market in the rest of the UK, I do need to explain a few basic differences.

In Scotland there's really no concept of a leasehold residential property. If you buy a flat in a block it will be freehold. You are the freeholder, there's no service charge and there's no ground rent. Of course, there are still communal areas and naturally these need to be managed in some way. Often this will be done by a "Close Fund". Let me just decode Close Fund for you.

Close is the Scottish word to describe the hall, stairs and landing, it will also maintain the roof, gutters and all other shared areas. Participation in the Close Fund is, in theory, optional, but it is expected. A normal arrangement would be each property owner contributing £50 per month, sometimes more, per property. If there's a block of twelve there will then be an income to the Close Fund of £600 per month, if there's twelve properties at fifty pounds. Often one of the owner-occupiers will administer this fund for free and oversee communal repairs as and when needed - perhaps the roof needs work or sometimes it includes the gardening. It's all very cooperative, collaborative and voluntary, and mostly it works very well.

There can be an arrangement where the various freeholders have agreed that none of them wants to take on the responsibility of managing the Close Fund because after all, it's a labour of love. There's no income paid to the volunteer doing it. If there is no volunteer it can be done professionally. In Scotland this would be referred to as 'appointing a factor.' Hopefully that demystifies some of the peculiarities of the Scottish property arrangements.

The property that we had our eye on was in a place called Latta Street in Dumbarton. It was a very nice, interesting property on the second floor of a relatively small block. The Close, in this instance, was only six flats. Five actually, before we started. Two on the ground floor, two on the first floor, and then one larger four bed the second floor.

It was a very nice stone-built block in a terrace with a central entrance door. As you went in there was one two-bedroom flat on the left and one on the right. You went straight ahead up some stairs at the back, which is very often the case in Scotland, up to the first floor. Again, the same thing. A two-bed on your left and a two-bed on your right. Up again to the top floor and the entire top floor was a four-bedroomed flat.

It was called Latta Street because the architect responsible for all the flats was Henry Latta. So in love with his street was he, having designed the whole street, that he decided to build himself a very special flat. His flat incorporated the whole of the top floor of this particular block. So, whilst every other flat in the whole street was a two-bed, this one was a four-bed. That in itself is interesting, because when you don't have many comparables, surveyors, buyers and sellers find it very difficult to establish a value, if it's literally unique.

There were probably between thirty-five and forty, two-bedroomed flats in this street and one four-bedroomed flat. It was a very quiet street during the evenings and weekends with a secondary school at the end of it. Our flat was opposite the church and there was also an Army Reserve training centre in the street. Residential along one side and on the other side was the church, Army Reservists and a school. It could get a little bit noisy during school going in and school coming out, and obviously the church was used on a Sunday, and very occasionally the Army would do some sort of training at its Army Reserve Centre, although really it was just used as a depot. Ninety per cent plus of the time it was a very, very quiet residential area, with some decent amenity space.

Typically, the two-bedroomed flats in that street went for between £95,000 to £100,000. There are a decent number of comparables for two bed flats. Our four-bedroomed flat, twice the size of all the two-bedroom flats, was on the market for £150,000. One and a half times the money for twice the space.

With this property wanted to do a title split. Title refers to the land registry title, so split this and create an additional title. In a physical sense it means to separate the property and create a new property too. All the structural walls and many elements that would be needed were already in place to do this because the whole block had originally been specified as two-beds. Henry Latta at some point (100 plus years ago) had said something like: 'Well, I actually quite fancy living here, so I'm going to re-specify this flat as a four-bed and I'm going to come and live here.'

We negotiated on the price with the vendor, we were purchasing this property from an estate, whoever had last been living there had passed away. They had moved out of the flat, moved into a care home, and then sometime later had passed away. A good tip for you: Purchasing properties from an estate, from the solicitors administering the estate, is a good way to get a reasonable discount. We didn't get a huge discount, but we purchased the property for £140,000. With a high degree of certainty the two, two-bedroomed flats which we would create would be worth £200,000.

We got the building costs nailed down tight. By this time were very used to managing refurbishments and we had a team of builders we trusted. The physical separation in the flat was just to brick-up one corridor. Everything else was a mirror image of what was below. We had to repurpose some of the rooms and the property needed modernisation. The scope of works was two new kitchens, two new bathrooms, two new central heating systems, some rewiring and plumbing then re-plaster and redecorate throughout.

We didn't need to worry about things like refurbishing the roof. Any expenses like that, the common area expenses, would be covered by the Close Fund, as would any structural issues. This provided a substantial amount of insurance in terms of other people sharing the cost of any necessary improvements.

Our total budget to separate and refurbish the two flats was just a touch over £20,000 and we were very confident that those costs, for the amount of work that we had specified, would be right. It was all looking good so far. We had a reasonable amount of property experience and a very large amount of business experience. The finances were all in place. We went ahead and purchased the property.

During that purchase process we got planning permission, which was not difficult. The council was very sympathetic about bringing extra accommodation into being and there was far more demand for two-bedroomed flats than for a four-bedroomed flat. Planning permission was quickly approved, and now we got down to the brass-tacks. In England, it's referred to as building control. In Scotland, it's referred to as a building warrant.

In England, sometimes people go ahead and start work without building control approval. It would be foolish in the extreme to start work in Scotland without having your building warrant approved. The building inspectors have the right to, and they probably will, come and inspect progress. They want to be able to physically see things like insulation and foundations. If you haven't shown them and you've started work without your building warrant, and you haven't given the opportunity to inspect, they are absolutely at liberty to make you tear apart what you've done. They can demand that you show them that whatever you've installed is in line with the building warrant that's been approved. If you don't have a building warrant approved you've got no standard against which to compare anything. The materials you use must themselves comply to building regulations standards that you might not have met. All of this you have to prove.

So, I say again, it's foolish in the extreme to start any form of work in Scotland, in my view, without full building warrant sign-off. Once you've got your sign-off, you will know the exact insulation, electrical standards, noise separation standards, air circulation standards and all the rest that you need to comply with.

We obtained the building warrants. That's where the problems started. It wasn't difficult for us to obtain the building warrants. It was difficult for us to believe what they were asking us to do. It seemed excessive.

But it was as simple as this. Unless we complied with the requirements of the building warrants, we might as well not have planning permission, because if all you've got is planning permission, and you don't have your building warrants in place, there is no point in starting. You might as well tear up your planning permission and not bother making any changes.

What was so onerous about these building warrants? Any Title Split is going to be subject to compliance with building standards that will be imposed.

First one of the proposed two-bed flats would benefit from what are called 'grandfather rights.' No more and no less than then building regulation requirements from when it was first built. In the case of this particular four-bed, it was built significantly more than one hundred years ago. In other words, there virtually were no building standards.

The other flat was considered to be a "new build" and had to meet all current new build standards. I'm going to keep coming back to this. It was a 120-year-old-ish new build. Imagine the difficulties of making a flat built out of stone with a slate roof compliant with the current regulations, particularly with regards to, for instance, energy efficiency and noise separation.

We'd anticipated some of this, but not all of it. The physical process for separation took less than a day's work. Some breeze blocks, a bit of plaster, a few hundred pounds. It could not have been simpler. Extraordinarily fast, extraordinarily efficient.

There were various aspects that we had not been anticipating. Fire separation for one. Of course, we wanted to make sure everybody was safe. In tenement blocks in Scotland it's not unusual to have a communal roof space. What do I mean by that? Imagine six blocks in a row of six flats. That's thirty-six flats all the way along the street and it could be far more than that. In terms of the loft space, if it is one communal loft space you could walk from end to end. It might be 100 to 200 metres long. You could literally go through one loft hatch, walk along for fifty or sixty metres and go through another loft hatch and you might be the communal hallway of a property that's six, seven, eight doors further along. The loft hatches do not open into the flats as this would be a pretty big security risk!

They insisted that we put in modern fire separation into the loft space and that meant we had to go up into the loft space and build two fire walls. Not one, but two fire walls. What the authorities are trying to do, over time, is to gradually, incrementally, improve fire safety, noise separation and all of the other things associated with improving the housing stock.

It did feel vaguely ridiculous to us that what we had to do was put two fire separation walls, either side of our "new" flat, when there were probably forty or fifty other flats where there was no fire separation in the loft space. That's supposed to be fair? Those other flats weren't doing anything. They weren't changing anything. For the authorities, when is their chance to make improvements? Their chance is when people have to ask permission to do things. Because we were the ones asking permission to do things, we had the compliance issues to deal with.

The fire separation was marginally irritating but not a huge issue from a financial point of view. Two breeze block firewalls one hour fireboard lined each side. It cost around £1,500. Irritating, but as I said not the end of the world.

Next is when it began to feel more than slightly irritating. There was some structural steelwork in the loft space. Steelwork, depending on the grade of steel, typically catches fire at round about 850 centigrade. So, if the entire block went up, at some point, in really crazy heat, the structural steelwork could catch fire.

Here's where I felt liberties were beginning to get taken. If the temperature in the loft space has reached 850 centigrade, the chances that everything else hasn't already been incinerated is pretty low, in my view. I make no claims to be a fire safety expert, I'm a mechanical engineer. I've got an appreciation of risk assessment, I've got an appreciation of the likelihood of that happening. What the authorities made us do in this particular case is paint all of the steel work with intumescent paint.

For those of you who don't know what intumescent paint is, it's a coating that will improve the fire-resistance of the steel by a significant extent. It's a bit like the stuff that they use to protect the space shuttle from burning up on re-entry. Would it have a marginal safety effect? Yes. But how on earth could that structural steelwork reach 850 centigrade without everything underneath, everything combustible, being completely, absolutely, totally on fire. Smoke everywhere. I can't think of a single scenario where that kind of temperature was going to be reached in our loft space. So, in my view it was absolute and total overkill. A waste of resources.

It was specified that we had to paint the structural steelwork with intumescent paint. Again, I hear you ask, is that such a big deal? Well yes, it is actually. If you've never bought intumescent paint before, I need to share with you that the small amount required to paint a few girders in the loft space was in excess of £2,500. That's without allowing for anyone to actually do the painting. So, you can see these costs were beginning to mount up very, very significantly.

Next, add to that the noise insulation and the noise separation. What we were required to do was break apart every single connection between the two flats. So, every time a water pipe, electrical pipe, or anything else penetrated the boundary between the two flats we were required to fireproof and soundproof it. Of course, most of the services did penetrate the walls, because it was built as a four-bed, not two two-beds.

Our original budget rapidly increased not because of planning permission, but because of building warrants, or what would be in the rest of the UK, building control.

Many people happily teach that it's entirely possible to make lots of money from doing Title Splits, and of course it is. However, what they don't so frequently share with you is that in order to do the Title Split there may well be a requirement to hit a building standard today and retrospectively impose that on a building that's one or two hundred years old, at eye-watering expense.

But we haven't yet got to the really expensive lesson. Let's just recap where we are so far. It was a BMV (Below Market Value) Property, from a size point of view, so we got £200,000 worth of property for £140,000. We got planning permission. We quickly got building warrants. But the cost of compliance with those building warrants quickly added 50% to our refurbishment bill, from £20,000 to £30,000. So, what we thought would be profit margin turned out to be us subsidising the cost of improving property in Scotland. I do understand it's the councils only chance to improve the quality of the housing stock. I do get that. I'm not complaining, I'm just sharing what I learned.

Here is the most expensive lesson. In the same way that the authorities considered one of the two flats to be a new build, so did the banks. What did that mean? At the time, in 2008, it was possible to get an eighty per cent buy-to-let mortgage and it is now, even 85% as I write this.

The rules for most banks buy-to-let lending, then and now, mean that if it's a new build buy-to-let the maximum loan to value on a bricks and mortar basis is capped at 65%. We could not believe that the banks were going to impose that. This was a one-hundred-plus-year-old new build. We had specifically asked our lender this question before we started and they assured us this rule would not apply, then afterwards they applied it! What they were saying was, 'This is a new title.' What we were saying is, 'Well, hang on. There's many, many flats in this street. There's lots of good 2 bed comparables. It is not a new build. This isn't a new housing estate that's never existed before. There's going to be some volatility in the property prices in a new development, but this was a very well established residential street, built before anyone in the bank has been born or even thought of.

We tried bank, after bank, after building society, after building society. They all said the same thing. Here's the next learning. Before you commit to a project like that, a Title Split like that, make sure your exit finance is in place and make sure the broker and the proposed lender understand that you are going to be creating new titles. In our experience this sometimes reduces the loan to value. We had relied on verbal assurances. Now we always want the offer in principle in writing.

So, what did that do to our project on a practical basis? We had expected to end up with two properties worth roughly £100,000 each, and in both cases we wanted to be able to put an £80,000 loan to value mortgage on them. Now we found out that for one of them we were only going to get a sixty-five per cent loan to value mortgage. So in addition to our costs increasing by £10,000, our re-finance had been reduced by £15,000. Sixty-five per cent of £100,000 as opposed to eighty per cent of £100,000. When we went into the Title Split project we were expecting to be able to complete the project, pull out all of our money by refinance and use our initial pot to go again. The increased refurbishment costs and the increased regulatory compliance meant we had to spend an extra £10,000 improve the quality of the building and, ironically, in return we could pull out £15,000 less mortgage.

Purchase price £140,000 and refurbishment £20,000 is a total projected spend of £160,000. The refurbishment included all the fees and a 10% contingency.

Then two flats valued at £100,000 each at 80% mortgage each gives £160,000. This would allow all our money to be recycled for the next project.

The final figures were £140,000 purchase price and refurbishment of £30,000 giving a total actual spend of £170,000.

The re-finance mortgages offered were 80% or £80,000 on one flat and 65% or £65,000 on the other giving a total re-finance of £145,000.

We were now faced with leaving £25,000 of our cash stuck in the deal. This was not our plan!

I'm sharing with you real life. I'm sharing with you real experience. Is property a get rich strategy? Absolutely. But you have to know what you are doing, you have to have the right support, and you have to have an expectation that it's going to take time. Property is not a get rich quick strategy. With the right support, education and mastermind around you property investing is absolutely a get rich strategy. In fact, it's a get wealthy strategy. Rich people have high incomes but typically no security. Wealthy people might have a lower income, but they've got absolute certainty that that income is going to be there for generations because they own assets.

Rich people have money, wealthy people have time..

Towards the end of this project we got lucky. Please don't invest in property, or any other investment strategy, on the basis that you're going to get lucky! How did we get lucky? In order to get some money coming in, we tenanted the properties as soon as they were finished. Then we started the finance application process.

One of our new tenants had taken the property just to see whether he liked living in the area. He was relocating to the area and had a wife and one child. He wanted our two-bedroomed flat to rent so that he could work and look around whilst the family moved up to be with him and then they could go house hunting together.

Within a few weeks he'd absolutely fallen in love with the street. His wife had come up and she loved the flat too. Out of the blue, unprompted by us, they offered us £100,000 to purchase the flat. This was a different strategy and I'm not pretending this was anything other than an accident. We'd had enough negative breaks on this project. He was our positive break.

At a stroke that gave us some "flip" profit. It took away the issue of the 65% loan to value on the new build, because they wanted to buy it. They were moving up from London, they had plenty of cash and were going to pay cash for the property. There was plenty of evidence the flats in that street were worth £100,000. They loved the quality of the refurb that we'd done, the new kitchen, new bathroom and new central heating. It was all good. It was lucky.

So here are the final numbers:

Total costs £170,000.

Sell one flat £100,000 and re-mortgage the other at 80% re-mortgage gives total cash of £180,000.

There was no tax to pay on the mortgage released of course. On the sale price we allocated half of all the costs to each flat. £170,000 divided by 2 is £85,000. The flat we sold for £100,000 meant a capital gain of £15,000 on this flat. We used both of our capital gains allowances that year for this flat meaning we had no tax to pay.

So, the final solution on that particular project was that we completed the project and we kept one of the two-bed flats that we had Title Split, and we've still got it to this day and we received cash out of the deal of £10,000 tax free! (£180,000 of sale and re-mortgage proceeds minus £170,000 of total costs). The flat we have kept has been a very successful buy-to-let for years and years, and there's a possibility that we are about to turn it into a serviced accommodation unit.

It's currently occupied by a long-term tenant who's in the process of deciding whether to move out or not. She moved in to the property in 2011. Depending on when you are reading this book, the exact status of this particular property is either going to be a buy-to-let, or it might become a Serviced Accommodation flat. We've enjoyed the capital appreciation and we've enjoyed £250 buy to let cashflow per month, or £3,000 a year profit, on it for years and years.

So, is property a wealth strategy? Absolutely. Let me try and summarise the lessons from this chapter.

Title Splitting is a great way to make money. As with every other strategy, you need the right education, you need the right knowledge, you need the right network and you need the right support.

Specifically when you are Title Splitting, make sure you know all of the costs, including new build compliance and anything that you might be required to do to achieve planning conditions with regards to sound insulation, noise insulation, fire protection, fire segregation and a whole plethora of building standards you are going to have to comply with to achieve new build levels of compliance.

Find out if the banks are going to consider your new properties to be "new-builds", because after all they are new addresses and new post codes. If they are going to consider them to be new-builds, make sure you do your assessment of the lending you are going to be able to put in place as part of your exit.

Had I known all the costs up front, had I known the lending criteria, could I have explained that to the vendors? Of course I could. Would that have had an impact on the purchase price that I'd have paid? I'm absolutely certain it would. You create value when you buy. If you under estimate costs you will over value the property and pay too much.

There are three points at which you can add value in any transaction. When you purchase, when you add value and when you exit. So I could, very easily, have added more value. In other words, paid less money when I purchased. I didn't know the refurb numbers, I didn't know the finance on exit and so I paid too much.

I hope you're finding value from reading this book. If you want to know more about how you could benefit from our mentorship so that you don't make all the mistakes that we've made feel free to get in touch.

Chapter Eight: Compare and Contrast - Lesson Three

In this chapter we're back in 2008 again and I'm going to compare and contrast a property that we bought in January 2008 with a property that we bought in July 2008. Two normal residential properties. The first was a three-bed maisonette and the second, a four-bed dormer bungalow. It's interesting to compare and contrast these two properties and the lessons that we learned. If I had my time again, what would I do differently?

Before we look at the first one, I want to take you back to the mid 1990's. Many people think that property investing specifically "buy-to-let" (BTL), has been around forever. That's understandable if you're reading or listening to this book and you are in your twenties or thirties, as far as you're concerned, BTL has been around forever. The very first BTL mortgage, BTL as an asset-class in fact, was only established in the 1990s. From the research that I've done on Google I believe that the first BTL mortgages were around the mid 1990's. 1996 is the first reference I can find to a BTL mortgage.

In historical terms property investing has been going on for thousands of years, even thousands of years BC. The Greeks and the Romans had property leases. I found this example of a lease for a temple.

> If today's property rental agreements may seem burdensome, the situation was just as problematic back in ancient Greece.
>
> According to a New York Post report, archeologists working in southwest Turkey at the site of the ancient Greek city of Teos have unearthed and deciphered 2,200-year-old scrolls that may be one of the oldest property leases in the history of civilization. The lease involved the loaning of land—including a gymnasium and holy altar—plus the rental of slaves to a local university. And while there was no ancient Greek equivalent of the Consumer Financial Protection Bureau looking over everyone's shoulders, the transaction came with its own regulatory requirements.
>
> "A guarantor was needed for the agreement," said Dr. Mustafa Adak, head of Akdeniz University's Prehistoric Languages and Cultures Department. "The names of the renter and his father were written in the agreement. Six witnesses were also necessary for this agreement to be valid, three of whom were the top administrators in the city."

National Mortgage Professional Magazine – October 2016

So as you can see commercial property has been around for thousands of years. BTL property, on the other hand, as an investment available to the masses, has only been available since the mid-1990s. BTL fundamentally distorted how the market previously behaved.

As you'll see from this graphic below until the mid-1990s there was a fantastically close correlation between property prices and the inflation rate. As an asset class property went up by the rate of inflation.

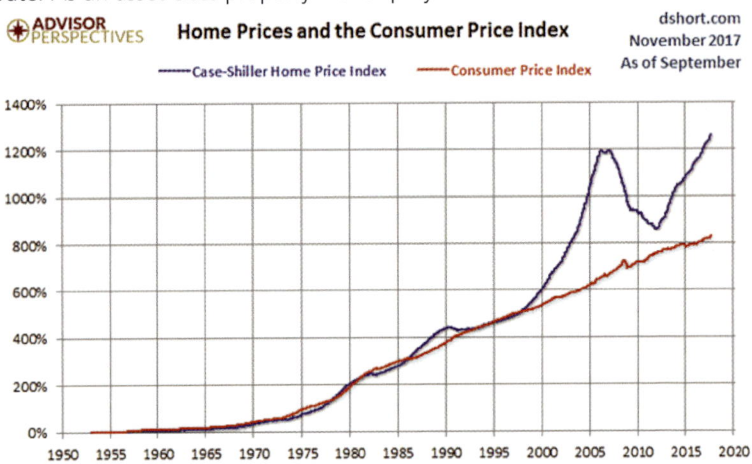

Now why is this relevant to this chapter? Well, I want to put it in to context, because there were other market factors to consider like right to buy, privatisation of the local authority housing stock, council houses as you might know them. These factors caused fundamental distortion which is still impacting the market.

The first property I'm going to talk about in this chapter is 1/1 Hood Court, Helensburgh. A three-bed maisonette, but an ex-local authority three-bed maisonette. It was in a nice enough area, perfectly safe, just three streets back from the seafront with plenty of greenery all around and plenty of parking. I wouldn't want to give you the idea that it's all shopping trolleys and burnt out cars. There was none of that. It is an acceptable area by anybody's standards.

Number one Hood Court is in a block of maisonettes. They are built two maisonettes high, so a four-storey building. It is of regular construction, not concrete or anything like that, with a tiled roof. To look at it most people would guess that it was probably local authority, or ex-local authority, but equally I've seen private flats that are built this way. It is just thirty yards away from the end of a street in Helensburgh called West King Street. Further down West King Street there are some expensive houses. In the part of West King Street that Hood Court is adjacent to the houses tend to be smaller and more affordable, but they're still private houses.

Why am I telling you all this? In January 2008 we purchased 1/1 Hood Court, Helensburgh with cash and we still own it as I write this book. We've had that property for years now, in excess of a decade. For the majority of its life it has been rented out as a private BTL to three different families. The purchase price was £70,000. We didn't particularly negotiate hard because we just wanted the property. We bought it for cash and we thought, 'We'll do a quick refurb, recycle our money out and we'll get the next one.' We had a litany of errors on this property, which is why I'm sharing it with you.

Ten years after purchase in 2018 (for both properties I will use a ten year comparison on their performance) the £70,000 ex-local authority maisonette is still worth £70,000. Zero capital appreciation. Now, if we dig under that a little bit, there are still properties in Hood Court being purchased using "right to buy". I did the research for this book and I can see transactions in the last three years going through at £30,000 and £40,000 with the huge discounts that long term tenants get when exercising their right to buy. So, when a surveyor is presented with comparable of £30-40k, they have extreme difficulty in valuing a property in an untested market.

Now whilst there are transactions going on in Hood Court and people are buying properties there, there are no valuation comparables for Hood Court. Our maisonette is a decent quality, recently refurbished property. The only truly established market value of a property is when it's resold privately, not under a right to buy. There have been two such transactions in Hood Court over the last ten years, but in neither case were these properties in good condition, they both needed refurbishment. Almost all of the properties are identical. The two transactions that have gone through that I would describe as resales, i.e. not the right to buy, have been £55,000 and £56,000. No comparables at all for property in good condition. Were these flats not in Hood Court, but rather they were a few hundred yards up the road in West King Street, we would be talking about £170,000 not £70,000, just because the address is slightly different. There are no structural issues with these flats. There is nothing different. It's normal construction. Bricks and mortar with a tiled roof. There's no fundamental reason other than address as to why the value of this property is so low compared to all the other properties in the area.

Now this isn't necessarily good or bad, it's just something to be aware of. What does it mean? It means that for a relatively small amount of capital, a relatively high amount of rental income can be earned. You'll see when I compare and contrast to the other property I'm going to talk about in this chapter, that whilst there's been no capital appreciation, the cash flow is very strong.

After we had purchased and refurbished this property we mortgaged it.

Our mortgage on this property is £63,755 and the typical interest rate we've been paying on this for over a decade is 2.25%, interest only.

The mortgage payment is just £120 per month.

The market rent we've been achieving started at £450 and by 2018, it was over £500 a month.

With a £120 mortgage and £500 rent that's a pretty impressive cash flow.

I suggest to BTL landlords making an allowance for letting agents fees, voids (empty periods) and repairs and other costs. Set aside 25% of the rent for all the monthly operating expenses which would include letting agent's fees, buy-to-let insurance and the inevitable refurbishments and maintenance. (Of course less needs to be set aside if you are self-managing). The tenant's have got the right to live in the house and when people live in the house things will wear out. The way that the rules are written the landlord pays for this. This all needs to be factored into the cashflow.

From £500 of monthly rent deduct £125 for expenses, the 25% I am suggesting, then £120 for the mortgage. That means £255 per month cash-flow per month after all expenses are covered. This is £3,060 a year.

How much of capital have we got tied up? The purchase price was £70,000, we spent £6,000 on the refurbishment and we have a mortgage of £63,755, so the capital tied up is £12,245.

Annual cash-flow of £3,060 divided by £12,245 cash tied-up is a return on our capital employed of 25%

That's a pretty strong return. Over the decade we've owned the property, the free cash-flow that's been generated has been in the order of £30,000. We've done a number of refurbs over the years.

How do the other costs break down?

Letting agents fees:	8% plus vat	= 9.6%
BTL insurance:	£140 per year	= 2.3%
Savings account (voids and refurbs)	£786 per year	= 13.1%
Total		25%

Over ten years that's £7,860 worth of refurbs and voids, which is almost exactly what we've spent. We did one refurb ten years ago on purchase that I will give you more information about later in this chapter and we did another refurb very recently with all the things that we have learned. So that's property one, in a nutshell. I'll go back to it in more detail, talk about the refurbs and other learning points that I'm sure you'll be interested in.

Overview for Hood Court, no capital growth, £12,245 cash tied-up, £3,060 per year of net income after all costs, 25% return on capital employed and repairs and a maintenance savings pot over ten years of £7,860. So not a bad investment.

Now, let's move to number 9 Maclachlan Road, again in Helensburgh. This is in a different part of the town, much higher up the hill and in an exclusively private property area. No ex-local authority houses nearby. Let's give you the basics on this one. We bought it in July 2008, seven months after Hood Court and we paid £195,000 for it. It is bigger with four bedrooms instead of three bedrooms. Larger private garden, a garage and a driveway on which you can put three or four cars if you want to. This time not a maisonette, but a semi-detached dormer bungalow.

You'd perhaps think that still wouldn't justify a value increase in excess of 250% in the same area, but it does. It's also much, much easier for surveyors to value this property because for many years there have been numerous resales at full market value because there is no right-to-buy distorting the market. Generally, the owners of the properties keep them to much higher standards and therefore you get less discounts due to the fact that there's less refurbishment needed.

We bought Maclachlan in July 2008 at the absolute peak of the market before the financial implosion in UK property caused by the global financial crisis. We did not spend one single penny on refurbishment because no refurbishment was required. The previous owners had left it in perfectly acceptable condition.

We marketed the property to find a tenant. We had an agreement with the previous owners who knew we were going to use it as a BTL and were more than happy to let prospective tenants come and see the property before they moved out. As a result, the day that they moved out the new tenants moved in and stayed there for many years. They were a lovely couple and they paid their rent without a hiccup for years and years.

Let's look at the figures on this one.

Purchase Price	£195,000
Mortgage	£142,467
Cash tied-up	£ 52,533
Monthly rent	£ 796
Monthly mortgage payments	£ 474
25% expenses	£ 199
Cash-flow Monthly	£ 123

Letting agents fees:	8% plus vat	= 9.6%
BTL insurance:	£180 per year	= 1.8%
Savings account	£1,297 per year	= 13.6%
Total		25%

The Maclachlan property has much more capital tied up and lower cash-flow so why would this potentially be attractive as an investment?

Lets just compare the returns on the same basis as before:

Annual cash-flow of £1,476 divided by £52,533 cash tied-up is a return on our capital employed of 2.8%

For Hood Court return on capital employed (also called cash on cash return)is 25%, whereas with this more expensive property, the cash on cash return is only 2.8%.

However over that period we also have to consider the capital gains position. We bought the property for £195,000 and the property went down in value initially. At one point, around 2009-2010 whilst we were in the depths of the recession, it was only worth around £165,000, so we had lost £30,000 on paper. I had a valuation in 2018 and the agents told me that there was very little on the market in Helensburgh and anything that did come to market was selling fast. Ten years after purchase the value was £265,000.

That's a £70,000 capital appreciation. We could release some equity from this property because it's now got a much higher value. I'm now in my fifties and I'm generally looking to pay down on my mortgages and move to a lower loan to value, rather than a higher loan to value.

So, whilst the cash coming into our pocket, after all operating expenses and the mortgage, is only 2.8% when expressed as a percentage of money tied-up, that's still at least two, if not three times the interest I would have received over this ten year period if I just left that money in the bank. In addition we have gained £70,000 value increase in the property value.

Neither of these approaches is right or wrong. I'm just comparing and contrasting. Investing in relatively cheap, ex-local authority stock with incredibly high cash-flow, versus investing in full price, private residential property which is going to be more expensive to buy, lower cash-flow but is far more likely to increase in value.

The other aspect to consider is how much of the 25% allowance we've actually needed to use on repairs and maintenance for the property over the years. We did no refurbishment at all when we purchased Maclachlan. None. The 25% for operating expenses was put in a separate bank account and you can see the breakdown above.

After agents fees and insurance we had £1,297 per year in the repairs account. The tenants that we've had have been exceptionally good, long term tenants, virtually zero voids and hardly any repairs.

Over ten years this repairs account has totalled £12,970 and we've spent nothing like that amount of money. Why? Because the tenants have done a far better job of looking after the property, which is obviously very valuable to us. We could add another £10,000 of this £12,970 that to the return for this property as well.

I hope you're finding this interesting. The comparison between two different types of property and two different price points over ten years. I'm going through this in some pretty fine detail. If you're reading this book it is because you'd like an insight into property investing from someone who has done it for decades. I think it's only fair to make you are aware of the different strategies that are available and the benefits of each. Ultimately, when you start property investing you need to do it on a basis that suits you, suits the amount of capital you've got available and suits the amount of time you've got available. There is no "correct way" to do property investment. There are a variety of options, many of which have got benefits and all of which involve potential drawbacks.

Okay, let's go back to 1/1 Hood Court. You already know that we paid £70,000 for this one and I told you that we did a refurbishment on it when we purchased it.

I want to give you more detail on this property. The entire cost of all refurbishments came out of the savings pot that we set aside over the years, and I would strongly suggest you adopt this practice too. Hood Court has always been amazingly warm. It's very well insulated and it already had double glazing when we bought it. The bathroom was fine. The property only needed a few things. It needed a lick of paint and it needed a new kitchen and some new carpets in some of the areas too. We did consider putting central heating in. The property is electric only and that's got some benefits if you're a landlord because, for instance, if you don't have gas on the property, there's obviously no need for an annual gas safety check and there's no central heating boiler to break or wear out. From the landlord's perspective it's often simpler not to have gas in the property. Again, that's something for you to think about.

With low energy electric heaters that are very efficient, there isn't a huge difference between gas and electricity utilities costs. However, you might see gas as a benefit to yourself or to the tenant. It's something we've done many times before and in some areas of the country there is still a grant for bringing mains gas into a property. Generally, we've found the cost to bring mains gas in has been around £350-400, although in the particular area of Scotland where we invest, we've typically had grants of around £250 to actually install the gas. So, it's not really a question of money to install the gas, but more a question of simplicity and who benefits from it. In the case of 1/1 Hood Court, the property is so well insulated that although it only has four electric storage heaters in the entire property it is still as very warm and the running costs are incredibly low. We've never had an issue with the tenants complaining about the property being expensive to heat.

These are examples of practical decisions you're going to have to take. Do you want to run gas in if it doesn't already exist? Are there storage heaters there already? If so, do you want to replace them with more energy efficient storage heaters? All these sorts of questions will come up. The decision we made was that we weren't going to do anything to the services. We just put a bit of carpet down, changed the kitchen and gave the place a coat of paint, and the property looked really nice when we were done.

We learnt some lessons when refurbishing the kitchen, too. Many years ago we were using Howdens for our kitchens. Howdens are trade suppliers used by a lot of builders. We went in and we selected a kitchen from Howdens. I wouldn't say it was a fancy kitchen. It was a functional kitchen, but with a new oven, hob and extractor. We also got a new fridge freezer and a new washing machine. With hindsight, would I put in any appliances? Absolutely not. We did it almost automatically, ten years ago in 2008, without thinking. We'd been doing property projects for a while now but we were fairly new to being buy-to-let landlords. So why would you not put in appliances? Well, as soon as you put in appliances, you become responsible for them. So, you're not only paying the capital costs to acquire them, if they break the tenant will then phone you up and say, 'oh, the washing machine is broken, can you send somebody around to fix it?' Suddenly you've got another layer of costs and complexity to manage. On top of that, we've had tenants in the past who have said, 'I'd love to take the flat, but I've got all my own stuff so could you get rid of the fridge freezer and the washing machine?'

There was a point in time when I used to keep my car in the garage. Throughout 2008-2010 it very quickly filled up with second-hand washing machines, fridges and cookers, and at some point you just think, enough is enough. And who was the clown moving all these things about? You guessed it, it was me! It actually got to the point where as well as my car I had a transit van, a big, full size transit van. I was just moving stuff about all the time. That is not why I signed up to be a landlord. I signed up to be a landlord for passive income and I have to tell you, the way that I was doing it in 2008 was anything but passive. It was a manual, laborious job. I was fitting washing machines. I was taking washing machines out. I was plumbing in dishwashers, I was doing all sorts of things. I also ran my day job as a management consultant. So by day I was "booted and suited" and very smart and by night, on with the overalls, monkey-wrench and away I went.

I was probably working an extra two hours a day or more messing about doing things I needn't have done at all if I'd have given more thought to it. I wish I had more guidance and mentoring back then on what basic things I should do and should not do.

I can't honestly remember ever having a tenant say, 'we'll take the property, but only if you give me a washing machine.' I'm not saying it couldn't happen, I'm just saying it hasn't happened as far as I can remember.

So, in went the appliances. Now, because we were providing all new appliances everywhere and because we had not yet learned to control refurbishment costs fully, we ended up spending £4,000 on the kitchen plus the appliances and another £1,000 to get a mate to install the kitchen. We ended up with a £5,000 kitchen. I learnt a big lesson from that. If you visit www.lnpg.co.uk, the Landlord's National Property Group (LNPG), you will find a fantastic trade discount organisation for landlords. Their kitchen supplier is Magnet and you can just go to a regular Magnet store, get whatever you want, show them your LNPG number and your card, and they'll give you a whacking great discount. A decent Magnet kitchen with an oven, hob and extractor (because generally you have to provide these) is around £1,000.

So, what did ignorance cost me on that first kitchen refurb? I'll tell you exactly what it cost me. £4,000. You've still got to the kitchen fitted but again, because the Magnet stuff is not flat packed, it comes assembled, it's a couple of days work for someone to put in a kitchen if they know what they're doing and you've got the right contacts. For an installed kitchen you're talking £1,500-1,600 instead of £5,000, which is what I spent on that one back in 2008. One of the lessons we learned in that refurb!

There's no refurb comparison with number Maclachlan because there was no refurb. That in itself is a lesson as people will say 'oh, you need to buy distressed properties below market value.' You can and that's absolutely a valid strategy. But if you're not interested in being Bob the Builder or getting a load of trades in and doing a load of work, there is something to be said for buying properties that don't need a refurb. If you don't need to do any work, then there's no project that could possibly go wrong. I'm not saying it's what you should do, I'm just saying please consider these things when you make a property strategy choice.

Now, onto the next lesson that Hood Court taught me. I bought the property for cash because I wanted to recycle my cash quickly by getting a mortgage once the refurb was done. The plan was to do the refurb, get a tenant in and get a mortgage. I was aware that a six-month rule existed, whereby most banks and building societies won't let you place a new mortgage on a property for six months after you get the first mortgage, but as I didn't have an original mortgage, I thought this wouldn't apply to me. This whole process is called re-mortgaging.

As I didn't have a mortgage, I thought I could go along to the bank and get a mortgage when I was ready. However, when I enquired they said to me, 'no sir, you can't get a mortgage for six months because you only just bought the property.' I said, 'well that's ridiculous, I don't have a mortgage.' They said, 'well you do sir.' Sorry? I've got a mortgage? How have I got a mortgage? They said, 'oh yes, you do sir, you've got an unencumbered mortgage.' That was the most ridiculous drivel I'd ever heard in my life.

So I couldn't re-mortgage the property for six months. As a result, we didn't buy the next property until July because as far as the banks were concerned:

I was "re-mortgaging", even though I didn't have a mortgage.

To this day I still can't get my head around that one. But I now know, it's important to understand that the six month rule is this: you won't be able to get a buy-to-let loan from a regular bank or building society, (although there are exceptions, some will let you do it after four months) for six months after you've bought the property, even if, as we did in this case, you bought with cash. While I'm writing this book I'm still shaking my head because I still can't believe that's the rule, but it's the rule. This issue obviously didn't apply to Maclachlan because we bought that with a mortgage.

What else do we need to compare and contrast? Well, the other thing we need to consider is the types of tenant and how we actually benefited from different kinds of tenants in different ways during this period.

In Maclachlan, as I said, for many, many years we had a tenants that stayed there. In fact, we had two tenants because our very first tenants, we hadn't expected this, but it was a very nice thing, were my oldest daughter, Becci, and her husband Kenny, our wonderful son-in-law. Roll the clock forward ten years and they've now got a beautiful daughter, my Granddaughter, Darcy-May Vera. So, hello to Darcy-May Vera, you're in Granddad's book!

Kenny and Becci stayed at Maclachlan for a few years and after that we got in really long-term tenants. Obviously, it would be unlikely that you'd get any trouble from tenants if they're your daughter and son-in-law! Becci and Kenny paid the rent on time every month and it felt good to put a roof over my daughter and son-in-law's heads. Then they went off to buy their own property, which is a different story. In fact, it's a very interesting story because twice now, for both Becci my oldest daughter and Jack, my oldest son, we've been able to help provide them with a house without the need for a deposit, in such a way that it hasn't cost us anything. Again that's a different story for a different day.

Coming back to Maclachlan and Hood Court and their respective tenants. At Machlachlan we had two sets of private tenants for seven years. For seven years we spent no maintenance money whatsoever on the property, the tenants looked after it wonderfully and even made various improvements. They had no "entitlement culture", they expected to maintain the house themselves and they did. Then in 2015, we turned the property from a BTL into a Serviced Accommodation (SA) property. It's been a great SA for the last three years because it's a good quality house in a desirable area. Briefly SA is taking a normal flat or house and renting to guests on sites like Airbnb and Booking.com by the night, by the week or by the month. For example we have families attending weddings as Helensburgh is close to Loch Lomond which has many wedding venues. It is also very appealing to contractors who work on the Navy Base close to us Faslane. 8,000 people work at Faslane. I'm not going to go into detail in this book about SA. If you want to learn more about SA I recommend you read my number one best-selling book "The Serviced Accommodation Success Manual" available on Amazon.

The cash-flow for Maclachlan went from £123 per month as BTL, all the way up to £2,500 per month profit, after all costs as SA (Serviced Accommodation). £30,000 per year profit from one house.

We simply couldn't convert to SA at Hood Court. It wouldn't command that kind of premium. So, the more expensive, the more prestigious properties, sometimes have benefits that are just not obtainable with the cheaper, ex-local authority properties.

At Maclachlan we didn't actually do a refurb at all until we'd owned this property for almost ten years. We did a refurb in March 2018 and it was more than just a refurb, it was an improvement. We added an additional shower room upstairs, completely redecorated, put down new flooring and put in brand new furniture, because now it's SA we provide everything. It's a hotel standard SA. We provide beds, bedding and towels all the way down to forks, spoons and televisions, literally everything. Guests just need to pack clothes and come and stay with us.

The refurb for Maclachlan in March 2018 involved complete redecoration. We put in a new kitchen, all new appliances, a completely new bathroom downstairs, and turned the upstairs toilet into a proper shower room. We also put a new boiler in for the central heating. So it was a complete refurb. Because we now know about LNPG, the actual refurb, bearing in mind this is a four-bedroom house and it was a big refurb, cost just £7,000. Then we spent another £5,000 on brand new furniture. The total for the refurb and refit and new furniture,new television, new fridges and freezers, everything you need to run a serviced accommodation business, was £12,000. Over the years, if you recall, we'd saved up £12,970 to our savings account. We now used this money to set up SA that'll be absolutely perfect for the next ten years.

Now let's look at Hood Court. We were putting money away every month and had saved up £7,860. Not only did we do a £6,000 plus refurb when we first took possession of it, subsequently, because of the way in which the tenants looked after it, or in fact more accurately didn't look after it, we had to do a second £5,000 refurb halfway through the term and more recently we had to give it another lick of paint. So what had the tenants done to it? Well, one tenant claimed that there was a damp problem, as the house was completely covered in black mould. We discovered the actual problem was that they would dry all their clothes on the storage heaters, which they shouldn't have been doing anyway, and they never opened any windows. In the bathroom there was an extractor fan and they'd turned it off. The humidity in there would have been 90% plus all the time. Their diagnosis of the issue was that it was a damp problem, so we were sending out damp surveyors, spending our money when really there was absolutely nothing wrong.

We moved that tenant to another one of our properties while we fixed Hood Court and guess what, the property they moved to suddenly became absolutely overrun with black mould too. I'm not saying that it's the tenant's fault, maybe they needed some education but we ended up footing the bill. We also had to do things like replace the work-surface in the kitchen when one tenant moved out. Why? Well, because they'd taken a pan straight off the hob and put it onto the work surface and it melted it. It was just lack of consideration. Can you actually withhold deposits and make tenants pay for that kind of thing? Well, it's very hard. Often it will just be classed as wear and tear. The tenant's deposit protection scheme, and your letting agent will make you produce evidence. Often if someone's been living in the property for two or three years then damage to the work surface like that is just "fair wear and tear". Sometimes you just have to take it on the chin.

So it's over to you now for your decision. Would you rather have cheaper properties with much lower capital appreciation but much higher cash-flow, or would you rather have fewer, more expensive properties that tend to attract a better quality of tenant? I'm not saying they always will. It's perfectly possible that you could get a tenant in an expensive property that doesn't look after it properly, but in my experience it's less likely. So that, my friends, is the end of this chapter. The tale of two houses.

Hood Court: cheap, high cashflow and still a great investment. or

Maclachlan: two and a half, almost three times more expensive, less cashflow but good capital appreciation and now a fantastic performance as a Serviced Apartment.

Just to bring you up to date as to what we're doing with Hood Court now. Well, we've just done the third refurbishment on it and we've fitted it out with furniture. It looks like we're just about to sign up with a company who are working at the Navy Base and they want to take Hood Court for the next five years and we're just negotiating on price.

So sometimes a little twist to the strategy, in this case working with local companies which we do for our SA, and you will find clients that want properties for many, many years. With this approach you're usually going to end up with a hybrid between BTL rental value and SA income. As SA I'm not convinced Hood Court would work because of the perception of the area that it's in. It's perfectly safe, but it's not always that easy to get clients to come into SA in ex-local authority areas. It is possible, and we do it with some properties. A typical SA (Airbnb or Booking.com) night rate might be £100 per night or £3,000 per month for a company. If the company knows they are going to use the property for years, they will negotiate say £850-900 per month. This is a good amount more than the going BTL rent of around £500 per month. So although it's a lot less than the potential SA rate, it's guaranteed rent for years, which makes it an attractive deal.

What I'm trying to do through this book is to give you as many insights, options and possibilities, so that your property investment journey is as rich and rewarding as it possibly can be. I hope you enjoyed my Tale of Two Houses and I'll see you in the next chapter.

Chapter Nine: Going Legal! Lesson Four

This next "Six of The Best" project I'm going to talk about was, in many ways, a wonderful project and in some ways provided huge learnings. I'm going back quite a few years to one of the commercial properties that I invested in using my Self-Invested Personal Pension (SIPP). I often talk to groups of property investors about the various ways in which a SIPP, or a Small Self-Administered Scheme (SSAS) can be used to generate very good returns for their pensions from commercial property.

Not many people that I talk to are initially aware that they can, in fact, take control of their SIPP or their SSAS simply by either starting one or, indeed, transferring a pre-existing company pension into it. This is precisely what I did in the year 2000.

I had a decent amount of years of experience in commercial property investing using, in my case, my SIPP. My SIPP had cash available and I had decided that I wanted to invest it into commercial property. Very briefly, I could also have invested that money into stocks and shares or precious metals or other allowable investment vehicles. To be clear, pensions, a SIPP or a SSAS, cannot hold residential property, only commercial.

This particular opportunity came to me through the distressed assets division of a bank.

I'd been in contact with the bank over the years about other properties and opportunities, and this one was brought to me by one of my contacts. At first it was not an obvious deal to do, there was bankruptcy involved. It's very important to be clear about the difference between the business in the property being bankrupt, and the owner of the property being bankrupt. With commercial property it's almost always the case that the tenant is not the owner.

Once I'd unravelled the bits of information that had been sent to me, yes, there was a bankruptcy, but the bankrupt was the owner of the property. I didn't get the full background details but unfortunately it sounds like there'd been a divorce and money was tight. There'd been money spent on legal bills fighting with each other, instead of resolving whatever needs to be resolved without undue financial expense.

I do understand the complications of divorce. I've been divorced, Aniko's been divorced, and it's a very expensive and sometimes traumatic process if one or other, or both indeed, of the couple resort to legal action. It was particularly ironic, therefore, in this particular case that the property I was being offered was a solicitor's office. So my SIPP did its due diligence, and I purchased this solicitor's office. The purchase price was a very modest £66,000. You can get absolute bargains on commercial property. Especially in a situation involving bankruptcy and the distressed assets division of the bank.

So the purchase price was £66,000 and the solicitor occupying the premises, who had done so for many years, was on a commercial lease. The income to my pension fund from the lease was £9,000 a year. So, £66,000 pounds in order to buy an income stream of £9,000 a year.

This is 13.6% yield for this commercial property bought for cash in my pension.

It was a four-storey office, a classic, "shop and upper parts". The whole ground floor of this particular building was mixed commercial occupation. There was a vet, a chemist and then the one that I bought. On the ground floor of my property was a solicitor's office and above it, there was what had clearly been in the past three one-bedroom flats but had been converted over time to become even larger premises for this particular solicitor to occupy. We own the entire four storey's of the gable and two units wide on the ground floor.

It didn't need much imagination to see that should anything ever happen to the solicitor one of my exit routes, because I'm always looking for multiple exit routes, would be to convert the building into five flats. This is a property strategy known as commercial conversion. I'll share with you shortly what we actually ended up doing with the property after the solicitor moved out, but first, more details on the purchase.

Relatively unusually, this commercial property was not on an FRI lease (Full Repairing and Insuring lease), it was on an IRO, (Internal Repairing Only lease). This meant that the landlord was responsible for the "envelope of the building", the roof, the walls and the windows, effectively to keep it wind and water tight. The tenant remained responsible for all of the internal repairs required, as well as normal arrangements for paying insurance and for paying the rent on time and any other normal obligations that any commercial tenant would have.

This particular case was interesting. The landlord, who had gone bankrupt, had been delinquent in his obligations to keep the outer envelope intact, significant water leaks had occurred. All the water had come in through the roof, because of a failure to maintain the roof. The solicitor, being the occupant, was fully aware of the rights under the lease (of course!) and because the landlord had been delinquent in his duties, the tenant was, not unreasonably in my view, withholding any rent until such a time that the roof repairs were made. So a "Mexican Standoff", in property terms with a firm of solicitors.

Why is this all relevant? Well, the £66,000 purchase price against the £9,000 per year rental income is a pretty strong yield. It's a good return on investment, 13.6% return on your money every year.

The rent arrears, the requirement to have the roof repaired and the bankruptcy were putting off a lot of prospective purchasers.

It's often the case that there's a complete bargain to be had if your level of knowledge, skills and expertise is superior to the average property investor's. You can see the deals where others can't. We already had five BTL flats at that time in this street and that meant that we were very familiar with maintenance, roof repairs and the other things that this particular block needed doing to it.

We asked our very friendly roofer, who'd supported our property business for many years, to go and have a look at the roof for us. He's now retired, hope you enjoy your retirement, Gus! In order to get access to this property's roof many investors were thinking about scaffolding or cherry-pickers or other expensive solutions. Not Gus. Gus just went through the loft hatch of one of our properties, out the access window and on to the roof. Bear in mind that this block is four storeys high, that's quite a long way off the ground. He used a harness and did this all the time in this area.

Gus, very quickly, very securely and very cheaply, went out to inspect the roof. He quickly came back with the good news that it was just a piece of lead valley gutter that had perished. He estimated total repairs, which he was happy to do as soon as we bought the property, for £250.

Which puzzle did this news unlock? As soon as the landlord's obligations, fixing the roof, were attended to, the solicitor would have no basis on which to withhold the rent. At that particular point in time £9,000 of rent arrears. I knew that once my pension bought the property for £66,000 we would very quickly get a cheque into the pension's account, for £9,000.

What most people saw as an onerous liability, I saw as an £8,750 opportunity. Give Gus the roofer £250 and then within a few days of getting the keys my pension fund would get the cheque of £9,000 for rent arrears from the solicitor.

I did double check with the solicitor before purchase that all of this would be in order. I explained that I was potentially his new landlord and that I would be very happy to organise the roof repairs, which the previous landlord had failed to do. He made it absolutely clear that as soon as I had done that, he would release the rent that he was holding into my account and all would be well.

That was the acquisition and it went very smoothly. The money was paid over, and it became part of my SIPP. £66,000 went out, plus very low purchase costs – the conveyancing was a few hundred pounds and another few hundred pounds costs went to my SIPP administrators – and within two weeks of purchase £9,000 of rent arrears came into my SIPP account.

This meant a net purchase price of £66,000 minus £9,000 rent arrears plus around a total of £1,000 in costs and the roof repair. Net purchase price £58,000, rent £9,000 yield 15.5%.

Things proceeded very smoothly for a number of years and the solicitors were excellent tenants. My pension fund kept the envelope of the building in good repair and the solicitor paid the rent every quarter. I got to know the solicitor moderately well through a few meetings with him over the years and it got to the point where he said, 'Look Paul, I'm not getting any younger. I'm going to sell the practice to the other partners.' The legal firm in question was an LLP, a Limited Liability Partnership. It's not unusual for the senior, perhaps oldest, partner to retire and sell his or her share in the business to the more junior partners. Wishing him well I met with the junior partners. They were coming towards the end of their lease and had decided not to replace the senior partner or to take on any more solicitors and therefore in the future they would require smaller premises.

We talked about various options. Could they just retain the ground floor, or the ground floor with one of the units above? Could they return to me some of the other properties? However, in the end we all agreed that it was perhaps best if they moved along the street a little bit to find themselves some smaller premises. Then I could redevelop the offices or re-tenant the offices.

All this was done about eighteen months before the end of the lease. I was then able to submit planning permission. After consideration, I had decided to sell the unit to myself from my pension fund and convert the offices to SA (Serviced Apartments).

Pensions cannot hold residential property so when I converted the offices my pension could not own them any longer.

I did an exchange with a delayed completion between one of my property companies and my pension fund. To be accurate, this property is in Scotland, it was "concluding missives" (exchange) with a delayed "date of entry" (completion). To do this sort of transaction with your own pension fund it all needs to be done "at arm's length". A commercial surveyor up here in Scotland did the valuation for the empty offices. A fair price was agreed with my SIPP, it was all done according to the rules of the pension scheme.

It's very, very important that you don't accidentally end up holding residential property in your pension scheme, SA is commercial property. Confusingly HMRC views that flats, which is effectively what I was creating, are not allowed to be held inside a pension scheme, even though they're on business rates and they've got the planning use class as commercial. SA flats, HMRC says, are too similar to normal flats and houses and HMRC would never know if I decided to turn them into BTL. Given the huge extra cashflow and tax benefits and all the rest that goes with SA, I would be unlikely to change them into BTL, but nevertheless, those are the rules.

I could hold the property in the pension scheme while it was a commercial solicitor's office and indeed while the works were being done, but once completion certificates were issued in HMRC's view this would make the property residential. I had to time this exactly so that my pension did not hold any, what the HMRC could consider to be, residential property.

I had good, professional surveyors and solicitors as well as good coordination with the SIPP pension management company. That is not where the lessons lie in this project. In fact, let's focus on the other upsides. In Scotland, as I've said before, it's very dangerous to start building works without obtaining a full building warrant, right down to the specification of all the materials that are going be used. Again, given the time that we had in hand, we also able to obtain completed building warrants in good time.

Pensions can't claim capital allowances (which are allowances to earn money while paying no income tax) because they don't pay any tax.

We got the capital allowance surveys done so that we could claim our tax-free income once the conversion from office to SA had done. We could claim a percentage of and a percentage of the conversion expenditure. As a result, a huge amount of tax benefit was added to our company in both the sale of the pension assets to the company and in the conversion budget. At the end of this chapter you'll see a picture and all the figures associated with this project. The tax savings, that we were able to claim, were well into the hundreds of thousands of pounds, just from this one project.

Again, this is not where the lessons lie in this project. Eventually, if we roll the clock forward to the end of this project, our five SA in this block have been there operating quite happily since the early part of 2017.

'What then,' you might ask, 'was the problem?' Why did this qualify as one of the Six of the Best property investment mistakes I've ever made. Where's the lesson in this one?

I went to reputable local building contractors and obtained a number of quotes and narrowed it down to one particular contractor. They were a third generation building contractor, very well known in the area and they submitted the winning tender. The contract was awarded, and money exchanged hands.

I had a project manager retained to supervise the main contractor due to the costs for the conversion. The general rule that I use when I'm doing commercial conversions for this type of property is to budget between £20-25,000 per flat. In this case there were five SA flats, two on the ground floor and then a stack of three on top of the right-hand one. If you look at the property from the front the right-hand side is four storeys high and the left hand is just one storey high. The budget for this project was £125,000 and we agreed a JCT (Joint Construction Trades) contract. They are available on-line for purchase and I strongly recommend you use JCT contracts for anything above £40,000. It is often difficult to get smaller projects under a JCT as small or self-employed contractors are not used to them.

Here's where the lesson started. We paid our deposits and construction started. We then moved on to stage payments. Every two weeks our contract manager would inspect progress and every two weeks, provided that sufficient works had been done, we released the next stage payment.

The deposit of £30,000 was sent to mobilise the contractor, get them on site, get up the chain link fencing, all the health and safety and the amenities as well as all the other things that a refurbishment site or construction site needs. Inspections happened and the agreed stages payment was released. This went on for a while.

We received a call from our project manager, 'The main contractor is asking for early release of stage payments as they have some bills they need to settle.'

That is never a good sign. The amount of money concerned was not huge, it was £6,000, but effectively it was blackmail. 'We need this money, otherwise we won't be able to get back on site on Monday.' We did more research. We were trying to discover whether there were background issues. Were any of their other customers being asked the same? We had personal assurances from the two brothers who owned the company that all would be well, this was a complete one-off, they were just waiting on a large insurance job payment to hit their account which was delayed.

This is a very, very difficult situation to be in because changing the main contractor halfway through a project is never going to end well. After much consideration and soul-searching, we decided to pay the £6,000. On reflection we should not have done so, but always hindsight gives you twenty-twenty vision, doesn't it?

We made the decision we made and I stand by my reasons for doing it. That doesn't mean I would do it again, though. The next inspection for the next stage payment was another couple of weeks later and work seemed to be progressing nicely (note, I say 'seemed to be'). I was provided with pictures and updates and my contract manager signed it off.

Now, here's where the project really started to be impacted. We could see that the plaster board was up and as well as the fibre insulation behind it. I could see the electrical cabling (first-fix) sticking out through the ceilings. The next stage payment was released.

Three days after that the main contractor went bust with no warning. We were approximately £75,000 into this £125,000 project.

My contract manager started to panic. We removed some plaster board and found out that no electrical wiring had been done, they had just poked wires through the plaster board to make it look like wiring had been done. No insulation had been put in place, just little bits of insulation had been put in to very obvious places such as through cut-outs for light sockets. Complete and absolute fraud. We had lost tens of thousands.

What could I have done differently? What do I do differently now? We were using a JCT (Joint Construction Trades) minor works contract, which was absolutely the appropriate one for the value of our project. So contractually, we were sound. I'd done my due diligence. I knew the company and I knew many happy, satisfied customers of the company.

Their previous accounts looked sound. There is a point at which it's not possible to do any more due diligence than you've done. The situation, when it all unfolded, was that one of the brothers was effectively the foreman who made all the projects happen and the other one of the brothers was the salesman. What I didn't know was that the salesman brother had been hospitalised for a number of weeks and he was coming off his hospital bed to meet me from time to time.

Their operation, their men, still needed to be paid, but their sales pipeline to their company and the cash-flow that it brings in with it, had been cut. There was no cash coming into the company from new sales, only cash going out. Like many small businesses, they relied on future projects and deposits to cash-flow themselves from project to project. As soon as they lost that cash-flow, they were lost.

To an extent they had my sympathy, but they also had my money and I had a half-finished project. This, again, was a hard decision, but I had to take the decision not to take any legal action against them because there's absolutely no point in suing people with no money. Specifically, the entity that I had a contract with was their limited company, which was in receivership by that time. I had no chance of getting any money out of the receivership. I've seen enough receiverships in my time to know that the only people that realistically earn any money out of a receivership situation are the receivers. Any other creditors get very, very few pennies in the pound.

How could I have done that differently? What instruments could I have used? What lessons can I learn? Well, my next priority was to get the project finished and return to think about that later. So, I went and chose the "next best" contractor from the list, who was actually a sole trader who wasn't operating through a company and therefore couldn't stand behind the veil of corporate responsibility and avoid personal responsibility if the project went wrong. He would be personally liable.

He came in and, in the way that many contractors and tradesmen do, metaphorically "sucked through his teeth" and told me that many a thing the previous contractor had done had been wrong or inadequate. Well, that wasn't news to me, I could see they'd been pretending to work. Even though I'd spent £75,000 already, he quoted a further £90,000 to finish the project. That's a budget overspend of £40,000.

Again, he wanted deposits to mobilise his staff. Another £20,000 left the account, so now I'd spent £95,000 on a £125,000 project, and I was paying a contractor to rip-out work that another contractor has already charged me for. My contract manager was feeling pretty silly at this point, but it didn't alter the fact that I needed to get that project finished and I wanted to get it done quick, this was beginning to hurt, from a financial perspective.

Work started, and it moved quickly. Two weeks in and we were looking like we might have a completion date in sight in the next four or five weeks. I would personally go and inspect, meet with the new main contractor, shake his hand and thank him for the work that he was doing.

The following Monday I got a call from the sub-contractors because the main contractor, the sole trader, hadn't turned up. He liked a good drink and he got involved in a fight on the Saturday night at his local pub and was now in jail. The sub-contractors were demanding payment for the previous week's work. That's how most contractors work, week to week, and before they would start again many more thousands of pounds would have to leave my bank account. How many times could a simple project like this go wrong? What could I do differently?

I now employed my own project manager to directly to manage the sub-contractors and we got the job finished. Once again, there was no point in me taking legal action against the second main contractor who got himself put in jail. I didn't have a contractual term that said, 'do not go to jail.' Ultimately, he caused me a delay, but didn't really cause me any significant loss, financially. Despite the fact that he did and still does have assets, the challenge with that particular legal action would be quantifying the loss. I can't sue him just because I'm upset with him. I need to prove that I suffered real financial loss, and I couldn't quantify it.

So, what are the lessons here?

Commercial risk. There are no circumstances under which you can eradicate all risk. Accept it, or don't do it. The only perfectly safe way to do anything is not to do it. The only way I could 100% ensure that no one was going to go bust, or start fighting in pubs and get put in jail, or rip me off, was not do the project. You can't control everything. Sometimes, you just have to play the rough with the smooth, smile, nod, thank the universe for the lesson and move on. Risk will always exist.

If you want to build wealth through property, you're going to need to do projects. I've had many projects that have gone fabulously. I've had a few - six, to be specific, that I'm sharing with you in this book – that have given me lessons. All the due diligence in the world cannot remove all risk.

Do take all precautions. Use JCT contracts, employ contract managers or project managers to manage all known risks. Please note, risk mitigation is not the same as risk elimination.

Another lesson that I want to share with you: property is very forgiving as an asset class. Over time, even huge overspends like this are paid back. It's in our language: 'Safe as Houses.' So yes, occasionally a project might just go plain wrong.

This block, painful though it was to complete, made me good money as an office and makes great money now as SA. Typically £4,000 or more every month and we still pulled out £3,000 in cash more than

total costs.

Finally the most expensive mistake I've ever made in property is not doing property investment. If I had let this unfortunate experience put me off, I wouldn't be costing myself £40,000 of overspends, some irritation and a project that's a few weeks late. If I did not invest in property because of a project like this one I would be costing myself millions. The most expensive mistake you could possibly make in property is not to own any, and not to do any property projects.

So, there it is, my friends. The rough with the smooth. "Going Legal". See you in the next chapter.

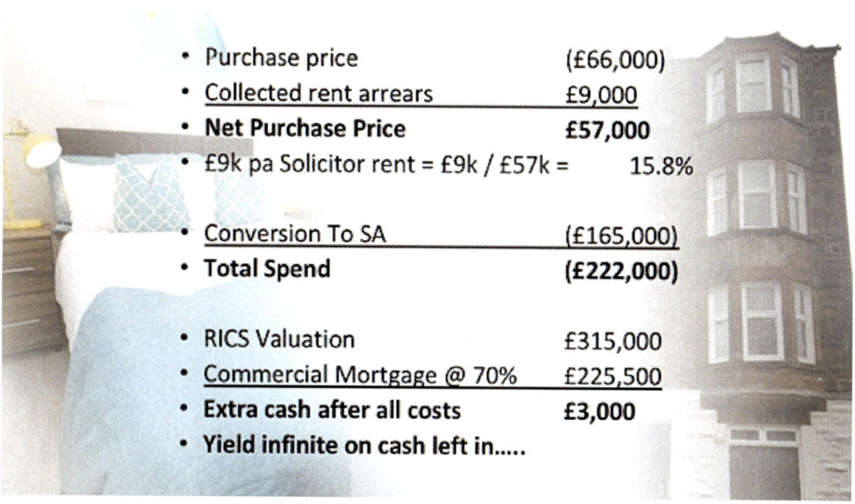

Get Started NOW

If YOU want to know more about

The Magnificent Seven Reasons To Invest in Serviced Accommodation

visit **http://bit.ly/m7report** to get your FREE report.

Chapter Ten: All at "Sixes and Sevens" - Lesson Five

A number of years ago now we started to build our HMO portfolio. Since the year 2000, we've lived in Scotland and the Scottish rules for HMOs are far tighter and more difficult to comply with than the English rules on HMOs. I better start by defining what an "HMO" is.

An HMO is a house or a flat in multiple occupation, hence HMO. Instead of letting out the whole property to one family, for example, it's let out by the room by the week, typically to single people, occasionally to couples, and very, very occasionally a room might be let to a couple with a child. Overwhelmingly, the demographic that uses these kinds of properties is single people.

Almost always, bills will be included. For a fixed amount of money, every week, the person using the HMO accommodation gets their accommodation, their gas, their electric, their council tax and their wi-fi. All of their accommodation costs are encapsulated in their HMO weekly payment. Apart from feeding themselves and entertaining themselves, they don't have any other bills to worry about. Usually, for a young or relatively inexperienced person living on their own for the first time, it's actually quite a convenient way to live. There are some extremely nice HMOs and some extremely good HMO landlords, however there are, of course, some not so nice HMOs, with not so nice landlords.

Now to the differences between Scotland and England. It used to be the case in England that under permitted development you could take a normal property in a normal street and turn it into an HMO. For the sake of illustration, let's say it was previously a three-bedroom semi, an HMO landlord might buy this and turn it into a five or six bed HMO. Each of the bedrooms would be used as an HMO room and if there were reception rooms, of course there would be at least one, perhaps a lounge and a dining room, those would make the fourth and fifth rooms. An extension into the garden might even create a sixth room. This could all be done under permitted development, i.e. the planners could not refuse permission and no formal planning application is required. Neighbours would not have the opportunity to object and as long as the property was not more than two storeys, no licence would be required either.

In many ways this light touch and lack of regulation has been a good thing, because it very rapidly brought into place a significant amount of extra HMO accommodation, which was desperately needed due to the housing crisis. The downside of course is that any environment which is lightly regulated, or unregulated, clearly runs the risk of being abused by unscrupulous people.

When I first came to England to do HMOs, I have to say that I was shocked by the lack of regulation. There is no "fit and proper person" test to be an HMO landlord. For up to six people, no planning was required and as long as the property is one or two storeys no licence is required. It used to be very, very simple to take a standard house and turn it into a five or six bed HMO.

Now, I need to explain further the difference between planning permission and licensing. Planning is predominantly to make sure that the use or the proposed use of a property is in line with the council's plan for an area, at least in some part, and mindful of potential objections from neighbours and other people already in that area. In some situations, the requirement for planning is overturned. One of those situations is this generic category of 'permitted development', where a permitted development allows for a house of up to six people. As with many things, there are exceptions. If a local authority, a council, particularly wanted to retain some vestige of control, they could introduce what's known as "Article 4".

Article 4 removes permitted development rights and requires all such proposed developments to be subject to a full planning application. On one level this allows councils to obtain control or recover control. On a completely different level of course, it introduces a huge amount of additional paperwork and bureaucracy, and it defeats the defined purpose for which permitted development was introduced, in this specific instance namely to relieve the pressure on housing.

It's not something a council would enter into lightly. Only in the most extreme cases in England and Wales from 2000 to 2010, was Article 4 even considered. However, as HMO density and the sheer number of HMO's on the market increased almost exponentially, Article 4, rather than being a measure of last resort, became increasingly common. In some cases, residential streets were being overrun with HMOs. The very nature of the street itself could change. Some streets, which perhaps for decades had been quiet residential streets, suddenly became full of HMOs with every other house having five or six single people living in it, almost to the point of that even if it were not students living there, the streets suddenly had a very 'student-like' feel.

I can well understand why local residents would want a say in this. Lobbying their local councillor for Article 4 to be introduced. Not only has the feel of many areas been impacted by HMO's but house prices have suffered too as less people would want to buy normal houses in high density HMO areas.

By 2013 and 2014, which is the period of time we're talking about in this particular chapter, Article 4 was not in place in Doncaster, where my next project was located.

I want to go back to where I started in this chapter by exploring the differences between English and Scottish planning and licensing regulations. The relevance of Scottish regulations is simply that we live there. The relevance of English regulations is that I had the opportunity to invest there. If you heard me talk, it would be immediately obvious to you from my accent that I'm not Scottish. I've just lived in Scotland for a long time. I was therefore well-placed to invest either in Scotland where I lived, or England, where I'd been born and brought up.

Now, whilst it was the case that up to six people could live in an HMO in England without the requirement for planning or licensing, as long as the property was two storeys or less, in Scotland it's a very different situation. In Scotland, as soon as it is more than two people living together who are unrelated, the requirement for planning and licensing immediately falls into place. In Scotland, for many years now, mandatory landlord licensing has also been in place, which has increasingly been adopted across the rest of the UK. There is an application process and application fee which has to be gone through for each landlord in each local authority area in which they operate or propose to operate. The fines for not obtaining a landlord licence in Scotland are significant.

For Aniko, my wife, and myself, for instance, if we proposed to operate in our home county where we live, Argyll and Bute, we need a licence each. There's a moderate investment in such licences, it varies by council area, but it can easily be £100, perhaps even more. That might not sound too bad, but what I didn't tell you is that this licence fee and the licence application process is not only per person, but per council, per local authority area in which they propose to operate.

Aniko and I, in Scotland, operate in three different local authority areas in Scotland. Argyll and Bute, West Dunbartonshire and East Dunbartonshire. We need one licence each per local authority area, therefore that's six licences. On top of this you will also pay a small fee per property to be licenced. It becomes a significant expense when factored in with all the other costs of being a landlord.

I do accept, and I think many people would agree, that landlords need to be regulated. We cannot have an environment where just anybody is allowed to provide accommodation for everybody. There's too much at stake. It's too important. People's homes, people's lives and people's safety are in the balance. I absolutely accept that there needs to be a "fit and proper person" test. I'm not sure I accept that this needs to be per local authority per person per landlord, though.

In addition to the much more stringent landlord licensing requirements and planning requirements in Scotland, permitted development is not allowed anywhere in the whole of Scotland. Every single Scottish council has opted out of permitted development. In addition to the burden of mandatory landlord licensing per local authority, the building regulations in Scotland are significantly more rigorous.

In particular, Scotland has a concept referred to as 'activity space.' To give you an example of what activity space means, if we go back to the subject of this chapter, which is HMOs, in England our normal practice is to have an en-suite bathroom for every bedroom. All of the HMOs we offer, and those I've developed over the years, consist of en-suite bathrooms with every bedroom to give a high degree of privacy and comfort. In England, as long as the person can get into the shower and use the other facilities of the bathroom, there are no minimum spaces. In Scotland, the concept of "activity space" applies. Essentially this means access for wheelchair users, so a turning circle needs to be provided in front of the shower, the washbasin and the WC, although there can be some overlapping. Please see the diagram for more information.

Figure 3.31. Activity spaces for accessible sanitary facilities

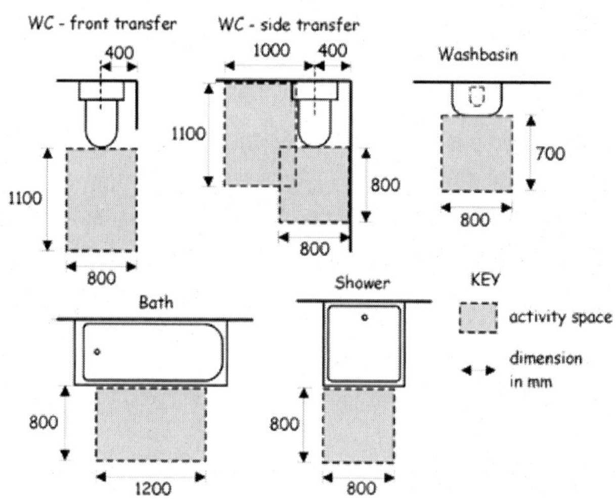

This means that an en-suite in Scotland needs to be huge compared to its English counterpart. In no way shape or form do I support discrimination of any kind, however this also includes discrimination against common sense. Activity spaces as a concept in Scotland apply even if there is no lift and the property concerned is on the fifth floor with stairs. Common sense tends to indicate to me that if a person is capable of climbing five flights of stairs multiple times per day and per week in order to get in and get out of their apartment, then probably not having wheel chair activity space in their en-suite might not be a game changer for them. On top of activity space in the en-suite, this exact same concept also applies in kitchens and potentially other areas of the property like bedrooms. As you can see, there are many reasons why we wanted to explore the possibility of increasing the cash-flow of BTL in England, instead of Scotland when looking to convert to HMO's.

Let's now cut to the heart of it and explore the cash-flow we're talking about for HMOs. These examples come from Doncaster a few years ago. I will refer to Doncaster from time after time in this chapter because that's where all of my HMOs are.

For a typical three bed, perhaps semi-detached or terraced, that we would take and turn into an HMO, the normal monthly BTL rent to a family might be £650 to £700 during the years that I'm discussing in this chapter.

Taking the exact same property, spending the required amount of money on it and turning it into an HMO, we would typically get five en-suite HMO bedrooms, each of which would then rent for £90 to £100 per week. If we've got five large HMO rooms, that gives £500 per week. With some smaller rooms and some bigger rooms, for a typical five bed HMO we would achieve a gross rent of approximately £2,300 a month. This total takes into account that there are 4.2 weeks in a month and the average rate we were achieving was a little bit over one hundred pounds per room per week.

Instead of £700, with the requisite HMO modifications the same property could suddenly earn £2,300. Now as a single let, I'm sure many BTL landlords will be familiar with these figures, by the time you've paid your mortgage, allowed for some voids and paid the letting agent, it's not at all unusual that the cash-flow from a single let is around £200 a month. The calculation I would normally use in order to account for voids, the maintenance, insurance and a letting agent, would be to deduct 25% of my gross rent (as per the previous chapter on this), and this would cover all known landlord expenses in most cases.

Although the income is much higher from an HMO, so are the costs. Don't forget that as well as all the other bills that we're required to pay, on top of that we're now paying for all the utilities and the wifi. For an experienced portfolio HMO landlord I would suggest deducting 30% to 35% from gross rent. For the first property, and maybe even the second, while the landlord is getting used to running HMOs as opposed to BTL, I suggest deducting 35% of gross rent. Put it to one side and then use it to pay the bills, the agent's fees and any repairs that are necessary.

Although HMOs do give fabulous cash flow, they're used a lot more intensively because you've got more people in them. Therefore, there's more wear and tear. To repeat normal BTL provides cash-flow £200 or so per month. This is typical across the vast majority of the UK.

Doing the same calculation with an HMO and the cash-flow increases massively to between £900 and £1,000 per month. Five times the cash flow from the same property when used as an HMO instead of a BTL. That's the essential reason as to why people like HMOs, as do I, I can't deny it. They offer a very, very high cash-flow, and yes, there is more intensive management required, but once that's in place, why would a landlord, all other considerations to one side, not want to enjoy five times more cash flow from the same property while serving more people?

Typical HMO income	£2,300 per month
Deduct 35% expenses (voids, letting fees, utilities, repairs, insurance etc)	(£ 805)
Mortgage (Doncaster typically £130,000 at 5%)	(£ 542)
Cash-Flow	£ 953

As many billionaires have said, whether it's Warren Buffet or Richard Branson, "if you want more money find ways to serve more people". Simple as that. Instead of serving two or three people in a family, serve five or six people in an HMO and you will intensify your profits.

We'll come shortly to what you need to have in place and the physical changes that you need to make to turn a property into an HMO.

First I want to make you aware of the law changes happening in October 2018, because as with almost everything to do with property, continuing education is required because the laws, regulations and licensing requirements do change.

As discussed earlier in the chapter, previously six people could occupy an HMO under permitted development without the requirement for planning. From October 2018 this will change to become up to four people. The government have taken a view that as most HMOs are five or six bed, this will pull the vast majority of HMOs in England and Wales into the planning net. Far more significant, however, are the licensing requirement changes. These change from requiring a licence for more than two storeys, to requiring one for more than one storey. Now, I need to talk more about licensing so that this is understood.

Effectively, the government is saying that unless you've got an HMO bungalow, the requirement for licensing will become universal. I know one person with an HMO bungalow, but that is the only person I know with an HMO bungalow, and I know a lot of property investors.
What is it that the requirement for licensing introduces to the mix? In many ways, it's laudable. It requires numerous extra safety measures, potentially even full-scale fire alarms, as opposed to just smoke detectors. It also requires one-hour fire separation between floors, which is a major job to do. It requires emergency lighting and additional fire-doors and many other extra fire precautions, all of which should welcomed with open arms.

Some of the requirements, however, are nothing to do with physical safety. They are guidelines , which are interpreted by each council. Specifically, part of the licensing requirements are designed to prevent overcrowding, which of course is a great thing to do. The piece of the legislation I simply do not understand, however, is how over-crowding can be subjective and council or local authority dependent. By the time you are reading this these numbers might have changed, but I'll just quote a couple of numbers to illustrate the point. It is critical you get the up to date information from your council before you proceed with an HMO.

One of the concepts in the licensing regulation is minimum room sizes. This is complete common sense. The minimum room size allowed in, for example, Westminster, is currently 6.5 square metres, where until very recently it was 5.6 square metres. However, in Doncaster the minimum room size is 10 square metres. Which is it? Is it 6.5 or 10, because a person is a person is a person. As far as I know, the occupants of Westminster are not exceptionally small and the occupants of Doncaster exceptionally large. They're all average, that's the nature of averages. Could you put somebody that's two metres tall or six foot six, into a room of 6.5 square metres? I'm going to suggest you might struggle.

Conversely, if the person is 1.3 metres or four foot tall, they'll find it relatively comfortable. I understand that we have to adopt an average in any type of approach, but how can it be sensible that 6.5 square metres in Westminster, or wherever, could be deemed acceptable, whereas to be deemed equally acceptable in Doncaster, the requirement for the same facility, a sleeping space, suddenly jumps up by over 50% to 10 square metres. That strikes me as absurd.

Even more absurd is the fact that local authorities can change these requirements. For an investor, just because Doncaster's at 10 square metres today, how do they it will not be changed to 11, 12 or 13 square metres tomorrow? This isn't encouraging investment into this sector. It's introducing a very, very high degree of risk.

As I already said, all of our HMO rooms in Doncaster have en-suites. Typically, these en-suites are at least 2.5 square metres, and some of them are 4 or even 5 square metres, if they are full bathrooms that we've inherited and decided to keep them that way. Incredibly, from my perspective, this 2-5 square metres does not count in terms of living space. The fact that it provides storage, the fact that it provides room to move, the fact that it provides room to dry clothes, is deemed to be irrelevant.

From a personal perspective, if I were living in an HMO room would I rather have, for example, a 9 square metre room with a 3 square metre en-suite or would I rather have an 11 or 12 square metre room without an en-suite? I'd go for the 9 square metre room with the en-suite every time. How can I talk with such confidence? Every time that we finish an HMO I've gone to sleep in it for a night or two to snag it before there are any other residents in there. I move from room to room, check the showers work, check that there are the requisite number of mirrors and hooks, all the other things that perhaps some people find a bit boring. What are you doing that for, Paul I hear you ask?

Well, I want to make sure that when the residents move in they actually have a good and enjoyable experience. I know the difference between an 8 square metre room, a 12 square metre room and a 9 square metre room with an en-suite, and all the rest, because I've spent many nights in them. I live in Scotland, our my main office is in Doncaster, and I will go and stay in my own HMOs just to make sure I am happy with them. I've got a pretty good feel for these different room sizes we're talking about.

Hopefully, I've given you enough background on HMOs so that you can know:

1. **The opportunity for additional cash flow is very significant.**

2. **Regulatory and compliancy requirements are higher compared to BTL.**

3. There's a high degree of flux and change in those requirements.

4. HMOs, this is my personal opinion, provide an absolutely critical element in the fight to relieve the housing crisis in the UK. I believe the government should be very hesitant before attacks on HMO landlords.

As a final footnote before I go into the details of this particular "Six of the Best" lesson, all of our HMOs that we built between the years 2013 and 2018, even though this was before the change in licensing rules, were built to licensable standards. As best business practice we will always future-proof as far as possible. Now, if something comes completely from left field, totally unexpectedly, you can't future-proof against that, for our HMO's we've done everything we can to protect all of our investments.

Now, to the project. Aniko and I, with our two local business partners, were presented with the opportunity to acquire a very attractive three-storey Victorian building in a road in Doncaster. The purchase price was reasonable, and it was a big house with nice garden to the back, fronting onto a main road. For the first time we considered going above six rooms. This property clearly had the potential to be a seven-bedroom HMO. That meant, very specifically, we were going to need planning permission.

We retained an architect, a friend of ours that had done numerous projects for us locally and plans were submitted. Without too much drama, planning permission was granted. What challenges did we have to overcome? Well, this particular property was terraced and even though it was large and had a front garden and a back garden, what it didn't have was parking. The main planning objection we had to overcome was the availability of parking.

This was a "blue-collar" HMO. All normal working people, not people on benefits. Factory workers, shop workers, that sort of thing. They were typically in their twenties or perhaps early thirties and most of them didn't have cars. In a seven bed HMO like ours you might find that one, potentially two, people have cars. In Doncaster specifically, most of the HMO tenants, our customers, either use public transport or live close enough to their workplace to walk or use a bicycle.

We made sure we had adequate provision in the back garden for bicycle storage and I believe we obtained planning permission so quickly with such little objection from the council or the neighbours was because just one street back from the main road there was on-street parking available. Chequer Road is a main road. You can park on it, although there are parking restrictions in terms of how long you can park for and time of day and so on. One street back from that, and the surrounding streets, with no restrictions parking available.

We obtained one hundred per cent "bridging" from a private finance provider. Bridging is temporary (relatively high cost) finance that is normally repaid when a normal mortgage is obtained at the end of the project. 12% to 15% per year interest is not unusual for bridging. As long as the project is relatively quick then this can be a good solution. We knew the bridger well as we had used him for a number of projects.

The agreed purchase price for this property was just over £100,000. By the time we'd accepted full bridging finance for both the construction and the build, the cost of finance was just a touch over £10,000 for a project that took six months. It took slightly longer than it should've done for reasons that I'll explain, and the scope of the works was very typical of what we've done for many, many HMOs, before and since.

To create seven en-suite rooms in a three-storey house requires complete and total replumbing and rewiring of the whole property, especially with the creation of seven new bathrooms. Each of the rooms was big enough that we did not need a communal living space, but we did need a big brand new kitchen.

When you're doing that level of work it requires a total strip-out. We completely replumbed, installed seven bathrooms, rewired the whole house and put in a new heating system. Typically, depending on the size of the combi-boiler, it's only possible to run three showers simultaneously off one combi-boiler, unless you put in big hot-water storage tanks, but that defeats the purpose of the comb-boiler. The rest of the showers are electric. In this case we had to put in four electric showers, plus the cooker, plus all the other household appliances, off the mains electricity. You need a good electrician to make sure that you don't need to upgrade the incoming electricity to a three-phase, as with a project this size you are at the limit of a single-phase electrical supply.

Sometimes, you'll find you need to upgrade the incoming cold water supply. With that number of showers running at the same time, toilets flushing, kitchen taps being operated, it can result in the requirement for more water than the normal domestic system can supply. Given that we ripped absolutely everything out, we also obviously needed redecoration and re-plastering everywhere too.

Very often in these Victorian houses we'll take out the chimney breasts, which most rooms will have. This will gain between 0.8 and 1.2 square metres of extra floor-space in a room, which is very significant and quite often the difference between achieving the minimum 10 square metres and not. We also installed new windows, new doors some roof repairs. It was a significant project.

As well as the refurbishment costs we allow £1,500 per room for all of the furniture; bed, wardrobe, bedside cabinets and pictures, and also contributions to the communal items such as fridge/freezers, cookers and all the other equipment for an operational HMO.

Our total budget per room, including the physical construction work, furniture, televisions and all the rest, was £7,500. For a seven bed HMO that's a total budget of £52,500.

Property purchase price	£105,000
Bridging Finance and legal fees	£ 10,000
Refurbishment and furniture	£ 52,500
Total cost	£162,500

As an HMO, the RICS valuation was £260,000 an excerpt from the RICS report is shown. This allowed us to draw down a mortgage of £168,000.

Address	Market Rent (MR) – Net - Assuming completion of the refurbishment work to create a 7 bedroom HMO, being fully let -	Market Value (MV) - Assuming completion of the refurbishment work to create a 7 bedroom HMO on the Special Assumption of Vacant Possession	Market Value (MV) – On the Special Assumption of Vacant Possession and assuming completion of the refurbishment work to create a 5 bedroom HMO being fully let at £24,500 per annum	Reinstatement Cost Analysis (RCA)
96 CHEQUER ROAD, HYDE PARK, DONCASTER, DN1 2AD	**£29,000 pa** excluding bills (Twenty Nine Thousand Pounds per annum).	**£260,000** (Two Hundred and Sixty Thousand Pounds).	**£210,000** (One Hundred and Ten Thousand Pounds).	**£150,000** (One Hundred and Fifty Thousand

All our money out, £5,500 extra cash and we were the proud owners of a seven bed HMO.

Where was the learning on this project and what qualifies it for "Six of the

Best?"

This was not our first HMO project and it was far from our first property project. I've talked extensively in this chapter about licensing and the implications of licensing. Whilst we very quickly got planning permission, that was of course subject to obtaining a licence because it is 3 storeys. We applied for a licence, and this is where the learning started, because this was our first licenced property. I mentioned it was three storeys, so we absolutely excepted and anticipated that we'd need to put in a full fire alarm, and we had budgeted for that.

The cost of the fire alarm was around £6,000 which is clearly an additional cost that we would not be subject to, had this same property been only two storeys. The fire and noise separation were anticipated too. The learning came in terms of what was allowed and what was not allowed for with regard to licensing.

When we started this project the minimum room sizes for Doncaster were 8 square metres. By the time the licensing officials attended, the minimum room sizes were not yet 10 square metres, but they had announced that they would be moving to 10 square metres. They were determined to assess it against the new standard that wasn't actually in force yet.

You can argue either way whether the council were doing the right thing or the wrong thing. From an investor's point of view, given that we were building all of our HMOs to a licensable standard and that many landlords that should be building their properties to licensable standards weren't, to be judged to a standard that did not yet exist felt very harsh.

We had long conversations with the licensing officials about what was and what wasn't allowed. I'll give you some examples. We had created en-suites. For reasons of practicality the en-suites, were placed back to back, almost like lift shafts, and above each other. The placing of the en-suite is important from a plumbing perspective as if you can put them all on top of each other, then the waste stacks, drainage and supplies are all on top of each other, so you're only running one set of suppliers through the core of the building. That is far cheaper than dotting your en-suites all over the footprint of the building. We completely avoid things like macerator toilets, which I won't go into the gory details of, I'm sure you can look them up if you want to. The traditional mains connected, U-bend, normal toilets are definitely the way to go as opposed to electrical macerator toilets, which are a) very messy, b) very unreliable and c) subject to significant amounts of maintenance.

Let's come back to the licensing. If you can imagine, you go into a room and if on the left-hand side of the door that you created an en-suite, you tend to end up with a 1 or 2 metre, let's call it corridor, to get into the room. The licensing authorities were disallowing this as activity space for the 10 square metres. They were saying that the 10 square metres needed to be in addition to en-suites and what they called "access corridors".

This was the first time we'd dealt with this level of detail with licensing authorities that were trying to implement licence requirements that hadn't even come into place yet and disallowing the whole of the en-suite and access corridors. By creating an en-suite we were not only taking up 3 square metres of space to provide the facility, but we were also creating an "access corridor" that's perhaps a metre wide. Now it's entirely legal to have an access corridor if it's a metre wide, but what they're saying is, it doesn't count towards the minimum room size of 10 square metres.

With this interpretation we were not only sacrificing the en-suite space, we were sacrificing the access space to the room too. We argued, and we argued successfully, that this was in fact good space. We had to make some minor modifications. We put in some shelves and some cupboards, because being a Victorian property the ceiling heights were high. This was now useful storage space, well above head height, and it became increasingly difficult for the authorities to argue that this was not in fact useful space. In addition to that we put in a coat hooks so that people could hang their coats. We also put in mirrors, so that people could check what they looked like before they went out or do their hair. It would have made more sense to us to put the mirrors and perhaps the hooks in other parts of the room, to provide better amenity, but driven by the requirements of licensing, we did things that were perhaps sub-optimal for the tenant, but which ticked some boxes for bureaucrats.

That is where I personally start to have a problem, because what I want to do is provide the tenants, the guests, with the best possible experience, not tick boxes for the sake of some "jobs-worth". It almost felt like they were trying to catch us out, trying to stop us doing the project, which I find distasteful. As entrepreneurs, yes, we want to make money. We're also trying to provide facilities and house a population that the government and local authorities have failed to house. Because of inadequate housing policies, failing to provide the requisite amount of housing, it almost feels like they want to prove that we're no better than them. It seems to be acceptable in the media to give landlords (often "rogue landlords") a hard time rather than trying to help them. We were clearly trying to be compliant.

I'll now take you to the top floor of this Victorian property. As well as trying to disallow access space and actively disallowing en-suite space, the next issue was that of space in the eaves areas. The top two rooms had eaves storage, which was very useful storage. The licensing staff interpreted that in the eaves area, unless you've got four-foot six clear head space, then that space doesn't count. We could put a chest of drawers and other useful items into the areas where we didn't have six-foot clearance. That meant very useful storage. What it didn't allow was for somebody to go into that eaves area and stand up. This doesn't mean it's not useful space, just because somebody can't stand up in there. They can still store things there. They can still have drawers there, which they can easily access while standing up.

There were many, many discussions and much burning of the midnight oil to come up with a solution that was ultimately acceptable to the authorities. What this forced us to do was delay the entire project by more than two months, which meant two months cash-flow that we'd been anticipating that didn't come in. It also pushed up the cost of our finance massively, because this was short term, expensive finance, which is fine if you're in and out of the project fast. It is painful if you're arguing with the authorities whilst paying relatively high rates of interest.

We were hit with a "double whammy" of two months of lost income and two months of extra bridging finance costs. Our seven bed HMO when full generates £2,940. We had tenants waiting to move in but they couldn't. We had an offer of mortgage finance but we couldn't draw down a mortgage, because it was subject to obtaining a licence. It really felt like the local authorities were torturing us.

With the benefit of hindsight, it was probably due to our inexperience. We have learnt a lesson from this. All of our prior experience (we've done multiple licenced properties since) has stood us in very good stead and over the years we've developed very good relationships with the council and the council officers. Of course, for all that I said earlier, mine was the naïve reaction of an inexperienced property investor.

What I now realise is that the people at the council are just doing their job, they're not out to get us, and in many cases when there's new legislation they're struggling just as hard as we are to understand it. In every case under all scenarios, working with people as opposed to having in your mind that they're trying to attack you, is the best route. If we can help them, they will help us. That is exactly what is happening as I write this book.

We've currently got a huge licensing requirement because our entire portfolio of HMO's during the period that I'm writing this book are going through licence application. This is because they are two storeys. Our planning and licensing applications are going through the process smoothly. Doncaster is my market, Doncaster is where our HMO's are, I can see a massive amount of other people's HMOs failing their licence applications.

What does this mean for us, in terms of best practice and in terms of picking up HMO business?

It's huge, because HMO's that previously hadn't required licences and are now failing, this is taking a massive supply of HMO rooms out of the Doncaster market. As the supply goes down, the demand for our units shoots up. We were 90% occupied and our occupancy is now around 95% which is frankly about as high as you can ever get it. As people are constantly moving in and out of HMO rooms and when you've got hundreds of them it's not possible to be 100% occupied.

We manage hundreds of HMO rooms. In addition to managing our own properties we also have a HMO letting agency. The most valuable HMO lesson we learned, which is the final part of this chapter, was to open our own HMO letting agency.

As well as demand going up, prices were going up. As I train many property investors and it was known that I had HMOs in Doncaster, many people came to Doncaster and started buying houses and turning them into HMOs and flooded the market. It wasn't ever really a big issue to us, because what they didn't do is spend the same amount of money that we spend on our HMOs. They didn't create their HMO's with en-suites. They were offering a different product, a cheaper product.

By the time this project was finished we had five HMO's operational in the Doncaster area. All the others were five beds. That took our total rooms - at the time - to twenty-seven. We'd been trying various local letting agents, High Street brands, people you would've thought you could trust to manage our HMOs for us, however it came to a head when our occupancy was nowhere near where it should have been. We were frustrated with other elements of how the agents were managing our HMO's for us. For example time after time we had been asking for copies of the mandatory routine inspections. When you have HMO's, as I said earlier, the cash-flow is much higher and so is the regulatory burden.

HMO's need routine inspections to make sure that fire escapes are clear, smoke alarms and fire alarms tested. There's a requirement to keep the public areas clean. I could go on.

Routine Inspection Checklist

Do you want to sleep well? I do!
Nothing more important than the safety
of our tenants. Weekly inspections are
particularly important part of running
HMOs safely and legally.

Download our inspection sheet here:
http://bit.ly/inspectionlist

It was probably the third or fourth time that I'd been onto this particular letting agency asking for a copy of our mandatory inspection. These are legally required inspections.

One of the more junior members of the team said, 'oh, I'm sorry,

yes, we'd love to do that for you, could you perhaps hand us a template so that we know what inspection to carry out?'

That was the last time I ever trusted anybody else with my HMO's, because although you can ask a third party to manage your HMO's, you cannot give away the legal responsibility you have. There is a named person on an HMO licence. If anything goes wrong, God forbid if anyone dies in a fire, if there are any regulatory breaches, the person on the licence is the person that's going to jail or getting fined. The fines are huge, tens of thousands of pounds per offence.

At that point, for that reason, we took back control of all of our HMO's. In March 2015 we started our own HMO letting agency. You could argue that we did it for the wrong reasons, the defensive reason to do it. It was a negative reason, in the sense that we couldn't find anybody else to do it to our standards, but it was one of the best decisions we ever made.

Our HMO letting agency not only manages our HMO rooms, of which we currently own 63 HMO rooms, it also manages HMO rooms for other people to an exceptionally high standard. Our wonderful team is routinely praised for their efficiency, for their occupancy levels, for the way in which they respond to maintenance requirements and for the efficiency of the inspections. We have been let down so badly by the failure of others we were determined to do it absolutely right. The next logical step, if you're managing HMO rooms in Doncaster, you might as well manage BTL as well. What started out as an HMO letting agency has now grown into a letting agency. We manage many flats and houses as well as HMO's, and that area of the business is growing all the time.

What started essentially to stop us going to jail and getting fined, became a profit centre. Even more recently we've started selling HMO's, flats and houses. We're now an estate agency too. I've got multiple people in the team that are trained as letting and estate agents and it's a fantastic thing to be the owner of a business.

There is always opportunity in adversity.

In this particular case, the threat of jail and fines has turned into an excellent operation that I'm proud to be part of, which makes a profit.

To summarise, what are the lessons from this chapter?

1. HMO's are an excellent investment.

2. They require scrupulous and timely management.

3. HMO regulations quite rightly continue to tighten up, to take out what the media love referring to as "rogue" landlords.

4. As a result of that continual tightening, it is more important than ever to be up to date with legislation.

5. Be careful when it comes to professional outside support, in this case letting agencies. Just because they've got a sign above the door that says letting agency, just because they've got a recognisable national brand, doesn't mean they know what they're doing.

6. Rather than getting frustrated with council officials, or other people that you might perceive to be obstructing your purpose, work with them and you'll always get a better outcome.

7. Wherever you've got a commercial challenge decide whether you can offer some better product or service, which as a consequence you might be able to profit from.

These are the lessons that I learned from this particular HMO. I hope you found them of interest and I hope you use them to your advantage commercially, if and when you start investing in HMOs. Thank you, my friends, see you in the next chapter.

Chapter Eleven: If You Think Education is Expensive - Lesson Six

Part One: Genesis

For my final project in the Six of the Best series I want to share with you what was in some ways my worst project and in some ways my best project. This project started in the autumn of 2014. The origins of it were that Aniko and I were living in Scotland at the time and we were working with two joint venture partners in Doncaster. We'd invested in Doncaster for a number of reasons. We still intended to live in the beautiful house that we've got up in Scotland. It's looking out onto the sea, has lovely grounds, eight bedrooms and it is the family home. However, there were a number of things that were much harder to do in Scotland, like HMOs for instance. Building regulations were different, laws were different, so there were business reasons why we wanted to be down in England investing as well. We needed a base somewhere and we'd established contact, friendship and relationships with two business partners in Doncaster. That suited me because I'd done all my primary schooling in Yorkshire, no more than ten miles from Doncaster, so I was familiar with the area, having been back over the years. I love Yorkshire.

So how did this property come to be known to us in South Parade in Doncaster? For the privacy of all involved I will call this Project Paradigm. To explain a little bit about our two business partners, they were an uncle and nephew combination and the uncle had hundreds of properties both single lets and HMOs. He was very courteous, looked after us whenever we turned up and he knew all the local agents. He was well connected locally. His nephew was much younger, twenty-one at the time, keen to learn and full of energy, and each of them in their different ways brought something to the team dynamic. As a group of four we did a number of projects together. This was to have been our largest project yet.

It was a Grade II listed building, just over 10,000 square feet, which had previously used as an office by the council and it had been bought as part of a package by a bigger developer who had eventually gone on to get the contract to win the right to build the brand new council offices in the middle of Doncaster. This as a project was born out of the fact that Doncaster Council, like many councils around the UK, is withdrawing from its spread of relatively small, diversified, typically Victorian and often listed buildings, and centralising for cost saving reasons into one big, modern, purpose-built office.

The developer in question had to buy the package of land and buildings. It wasn't negotiable. It was one 'lot' that was available for sale. Some of those properties the developer went on to build out or knock down and rebuild, or all of the other things that developers do. Some of the plots were just in that sweet spot for private investors like myself, and potentially like yourself, where they were too small to be considered for development by the bigger developer yet too large or complicated for private individuals. Bigger developers will often not enter into a project with a GDV, that's a Gross Development Value, of less than several million and most buy-to-let investors won't take on projects that are more complicated than a buy-to-let where perhaps the purchase costs are in the hundreds of thousands and so are the development costs.

You've got this sweet spot that's above the reach and complexity that a smaller investor will take on, but it's too small for one of the more established and bigger investors. Typically, these projects are one or two million pounds, perhaps up to three million pounds. The marketplace gets much more active for development above five million and much more active for private investors below half a million. The sweet spot, let's say, is one to four million of purchase and development combined. This was just such a project.

Now, if I take you back to Doncaster on an autumn morning, our two joint venture partners are parked in South Parade. The uncle went into his solicitors, of which there are a number in South Parade, to finalise some paperwork on a deal. The nephew was left on his own in the car just looking about. Completely by chance they were parked right outside Project Paradigm. It had been for sale for a long time, six or seven years, at just around the £600,000 mark. It had very recently been reduced. The nephew researched all this information and shared it with us. It was a gorgeous building. 10,000 square feet spread over four floors, a self-contained carpark and a little bit of land at the back. The views at the rear were on to parkland and a museum and the front looked over a desirable regency square with an area of garden in the middle. It was on a wide, tree-lined street. A very attractive building at a very attractive price.

A few months later we had an offer accepted of £323,500. Before we invested we had a lot to do. Due diligence is very important. How much will it cost to buy? Never mind how much it's going to cost to buy, a better question is, what is it going to cost to build it out and what can we do with it? Because clearly, whilst in principle we wanted to buy it, it would be foolish to buy it without first establishing what the development options were, the exit routes, what the build costs were going to be, would we get planning permission and many other considerations besides. In principle we had the offer accepted and we had a couple of months to get our heads around what we were going to do with this thing.

It was an unusual situation in the sense that normally it's pretty clear what you're going to do with a building, but this one was sufficiently rich in options that we genuinely did need some time to think about what our preferred option was. The first step was to go and talk to an architect. The second step was to engage a quantity surveyor to establish what the likely build costs would be, as soon as we got a rough plan outlined with the architect. The third part of the plan was that once we'd got the building, we'd got some architects plans and we'd got some costings, how were we going to finance it?

At that time, Aniko and I had been in a mentorship programme with a property training company and this particular property training company was very clear that one of the major benefits of its training programmes was the ability for the students to joint venture with each other, to raise private equity within the mentorship group. They also offered the chance for people like myself to train others in their programme. Now, what gave me the right to train others? To train anybody for that matter? I'd been property investing for many years by that point and we did have a reasonable portfolio of properties. We had single lets, we had HMOs, we'd done commercial conversions and we were investing using our pension funds. Aniko and I, as well as having first degrees, also had MBAs. I'd run companies large and small, I was well-versed with company structures and tax legislation, so this property training company took a view that I was probably someone that could be trained to teach others.

At the same time as we were considering our options to buy Project Paradigm, I had just started the process of being trained to train other people. I was running some very small classes and in these classes I was encouraged to share my case studies, ideally live case studies, of the projects that I was involved in. Naturally Project Paradigm made its way into my presentation materials as an example of a live project that I was currently working on. I was then approached by two fellow members of this mentorship programme who were also learning to be trainers in order to share their knowledge. They were qualified in different ways. One of them had in excess of fifty single lets and the other had done a commercial conversion and created office space with some living space above it. They both also had other properties. They were considered to be of merit for training and could pass on their knowledge and support others in their desire to build a property portfolio because they were doing it themselves.

I remember clearly, I was at the offices of this training company one morning delivering one of my very first stand-alone training programmes. I was being supported and assisted by one of these two other trainers. At lunchtime the trainer approached me, the one with the fifty buy-to-lets, and said, 'Would you be interested in me investing in your Paradigm project?' This took me back. It surprised me because, although we were in the process of negotiating the deal, we hadn't actually bought it. We didn't actually have a specific plan as to what we were going to do with it, but nevertheless I explored the conversation and within a matter of days an offer of £250,000 in private finance was on the table from this trainer/investor.

Very shortly after that the second fellow trainer and member of the mentoring program also put an offer on the table of £250,000 in private finance. Terms to be agreed, details to be agreed, but half a million pounds of private finance was suddenly available for a £323,500 building and I hadn't actually asked for any money. I'd been offered it twice. Many months later this process repeated itself. On this occasion, this was another member of the same mentorship community with whom I was delivering some property training in the Middle East. Again, I hadn't actually asked for any money. I'd been approached by the person organising the event in the Middle East. This time it was for a larger amount of money, £300,000. I now had pledges of £800,000 in private finance for a project where plans were still to be finalised! The element of raising finance as part of the due diligence was looking like it wasn't going to be required as we had so much private finance pledged. The focus shifted to drawings and plans. Our decision was that we needed to get the architect and one of our local joint venture partners to meet with the council.

Over that period, we as a group met with the council a number of times. Doncaster is a relatively unusual town in the sense that it has a special mayor, which of course isn't unusual, and that mayor is elected, which again isn't unusual. The unusual part is that the mayor has executive powers. We sought assurances from the mayor as to the type of development that would be supported and the answer we got back was as long as it was commercially viable, as long as it was sympathetic, it would be supported. We put in some outline plans. 10,000 square feet of office to residential would normally be 'permitted development' and as such wouldn't require planning. However, you will recall that this one was a Grade II listed building and therefore it did require planning.

We submitted a proposal for conversion to fifteen flats. There were many beautiful aspects to the building and there had been some modifications after its original build which were on the outside and were very sympathetic. It had a basement plus three storeys above ground and looking at it from the front, on the left-hand side there was a double height extension in the original style of the three-storey property. To give access to that area there had been a third staircase put in, which was not original and was particularly unremarkable. To maximise the opportunity from a GDV point of view, we asked for fifteen flats. That would require one of the staircases to be taken out, but this was the unremarkable, non-original staircase and not considered something historically significant.

In principle, both the senior planners and the 'senior management' of the council supported the proposal and it looked like we had a viable project on our hands. We got costings pulled together by the quantity surveyor for this project and with the fifteen flats the cost came back with a projection of £590,000. Now, you will understand that these are not guaranteed costs, but neither are they a 'wet-finger in the air.' This was prepared by a construction professional, a quantity surveyor, using their skills, expertise and knowledge to estimate £590,000 of build costs given that specific building and our plan for fifteen flats. They went on site and they did a number of surveys and together with the plans, in their professional view, they wrote to us and confirmed £590,000 as an estimate.

It was now time to start adding the numbers together in terms of the feasibility. To get this far we had spent thousands of pounds with the architect and the quantity surveyor in professional fees. It would be foolish not to invest thousands of pounds when you've got a project of this scale to make sure it works and to do your due diligence before you start committing much larger sums.

Due diligence is a term that you'll perhaps hear a lot. People ask, 'If you've done your due diligence properly, how come you got your numbers so wrong?' It just happens sometimes. I'd been involved in my corporate life in due diligence projects that have cost millions of pounds and yet the projections have been wrong by hundreds of millions. Due diligence is not a perfect science. It's an art, in fact. A basic scientific concept is this: 'It is never possible to prove anything. It is only possible to disprove it.' Of course, everything looks very different with twenty-twenty hindsight.

After our due diligence cost phase, the figures were:

1. £335,000 to acquire (including fees and stamp duty)

2. £590,000 to build

3. 10% contingency

4. Sub-total of £925,000

5. To that we needed to add the professional fees and some overall project contingency

6. The working budget was £1,000,000 to buy it and build it

What should we get for that? We should get fifteen very attractive, reasonably spacious flats. 10,000 square feet divided by fifteen flats is just over 650 square foot average per flat. We have to allow for staircases and hallways, but nevertheless, the average flat in that development would have been above 500 square feet or over 46 square metres. That is in excess of new build standards and permitted development would have allowed even more flats.

With permitted development you'll often see developers going down to 350 square feet, just over 30 square metres. The flats we were hoping to build were at least fifty per cent above the standard space that you're likely to get in a flat from permitted development. Plus, don't forget the gorgeous building, the views are stunning from both the front and the back and some of the flats at the back would have their own private terraces overlooking the parkland, and furthermore it had its own gated private carpark. We'd even included landscaped gardens and allowed for fountains and decking. Our aim was to make it a really lovely place to live.

Various estate agents were retained to come and give us a view as to the GDV. In total we saw five agents and the GDV ranges that we got for these fifteen luxury apartments was from a minimum of £1.8 million all the way up to £3 million. The plans included one beds and some two beds. The local estate agents estimated minimum values between £110,000 to £120,000. At the top end we had some valuations with prices approaching £200,000 for some of the flats. Having worked with five agents we felt we had a good picture of what 'worst case' looked like from the professionals.

Comparables were difficult because there are not many projects like this near to this part of Doncaster. There are some extremely expensive places in Doncaster, but Paradigm is not located in one of them. It was proposed to be a luxurious development, but slightly out of the area where it would have absolutely maximised its value. Nevertheless, if we take the most pessimistic GDV we were given of £1.8 million and the estimated total costs professionally quantified at £1 million, this was a viable project.

Review of key assumptions used for the proposed fifteen luxury apartments development:

Acquisition cost including stamp duty	£335,000
Build costs including contingency	£590,000
Various professional fees	£75,000
TOTAL COST ESTIMATE	£1,000,000
Valuation range	£1.8m - £3.0m
Private Finance pledged	£800,000

At this point we re-opened discussions with our potential private investors.

We had £1 million total cost and £800,000 already pledged, so could we and the other joint venture partners come up with the £200,000 between us? Of course, we could. Again, worst case scenario, could we put in a small amount of bridging or other similar short-term finance towards the end of the project? Certainly, and we had this confirmed by finance brokers.

Would bridging be necessary? Probably not because sales could start happening off-plan as soon as the development started. We planned to develop the two-storey extension that I mentioned earlier first, and had plans drawn up to create show flats in it. It was a self-contained annex and we could develop two flats there and sell them before we then went on to develop the main building.

There were multiple ways in which we could manage the cashflow situation that probably meant on a million-pound project, of which we already had £800,000, it was quite likely we would not need any more money.

The two initial investors who were pledging £250,000 each were hugely supportive and extremely keen on the project. The deal that was done with these two investors was that instead of giving them an interest rate-based return, we would work with them long-term by offering them one of the fifteen flats plus their original funds returned. Of course, this would still leave us with thirteen flats after we'd given the two investors a flat each. The third investor simply wanted interest on his investment, so we agreed an interest rate.

The two quarter of a million pound investors agreed to put up their money upfront and proposed that they take a joint first charge on Paradigm in order that we could purchase the property and get the project started. We shared with them the due diligence, the projections, the information we had gathered from the mayor and the planners and they were extremely keen. It looked like an excellent project. The third investor was going to take some time to get the funds together, so they agreed to come in after the property had been purchased and were content to take a second charge on Paradigm.

To return to the title of Part One: Genesis, this is how the project was born, how it came together. Sometimes you don't plan these things. They happen with a mind of their own.

Four joint venture partners, two local and two of us living in Scotland. A property sourced by accident whilst waiting in a car for an uncle to return. Three investors approaching us to offer funds. Professional input and a warm welcome from the mayor and planners. This looked to all of us to be a great deal.

We took the decision to form a new company, an SPV (Special Purpose Vehicle) to transact the deal. Why did we do that? You'll often hear me talk about 'fire-walling' and risk and never putting an asset into an operational business. Drawing on my experience, we set up the SPV as an LLP (Limited Liability Partnership), sorry for all these TLAs (Three letter acronyms)! We created a new legal entity that had no other assets or liabilities of any kind. The four joint venture partners became Partners (the legal term) in the LLP. Why an LLP versus a limited company? The main reason was the very significant capital allowances in the Paradigm project. What's a capital allowance? I've touched on this in previous chapters. A capital allowance is an amount of income that can be earned tax free as a consequence of purchasing commercial property and as a further consequence of then converting that commercial property.

For purchasing the property, capital allowances of £60,000 were identified. How did we know that? We retained a professional capital allowance surveyor to do a survey. When the development was complete there would be further huge amounts of capital allowances, many hundreds of thousands of pounds. The most efficient way to use the capital allowances for this project was through an LLP, not through a limited company. Why?

That is a subject for a separate chapter, in a separate book, on a separate day.

What other elements of value were there in this project? Creating fifteen new flats with fifteen new leases, ninety-nine or 125 year leases, would clearly give the freehold value. This was over and above the GDV estimated by the estate agents.

I'm going to move on now from Genesis, how the project started, to implementation. Those of you who know me have heard me say many times: 'If you think education is expensive try ignorance.' We were relatively well educated, and we certainly didn't think we were ignorant, but there were many things in this project that came as surprises to us all.

Part Two: Implementation

We now started to purchase the property. The purchase date was agreed for July 2015. A contract was put in place and this contract was with a big developer. The deposit agreed was ten per cent of £323,500 and inserted into the purchase contract, which we exchanged on. There was a very important phase: 'Time is of the essence.' What that means, if you've never seen that in a purchase contract before, is that if you fail to complete within a maximum of seven days after the date of the agreed completion date, your deposit and your right to purchase the building will be forfeit. So, watch out for that, my friends. 'Time is of the essence.'

The first investor moved very quickly and was forthcoming with their £250,000. We used some of that to clear the professional fees that we'd carried in the project so far. This included the solicitor, the quantity surveyor and the capital allowance specialist. At that stage fees due were to the order of £10,000, and including the £32,500 deposit, the total funds expended at this point were under £50,000.

Time moved on, exchange of contracts happened, and completion was looming. I remember it well because we were supposed to be on holiday in Portugal. What I was actually doing on a daily basis was chasing the second investor for their funds from Portugal. They had promised, and legally committed via a solicitor, to invest £250,000. They were part of our community, they were known to me and they'd made a promise to me, but the funds were not forthcoming. There were some very difficult phone calls. We got to the point where we had just one day, or we would lose the project, our right to purchase it, significant reputational damage and the deposit. Before we even started, collectively we would be out of pocket by £50,000 if the investor had failed to deliver on their promise.

Whilst this had never been the plan, Aniko and I in the background moved funds such that we could inject our capital if we had to. We had until noon the following day. Clearly, we didn't tell anybody what we were preparing to do and literally at the eleventh hour, by which time we had transferred our funds to our solicitors as a Plan B, I got a call from the investor to say that whilst they couldn't come up with the entire funds they managed to pull together enough to allow completion. Now, that should have been a warning. Anytime someone fails to deliver on what they've told you, you need to look hard, dig deep and understand why it is that they failed to perform.

We had a pressing need to get the funds into the hands of our solicitor, so they were passed straight to the solicitor from the investor and the solicitor confirmed that she had the funds on account and we were in a position to complete. This satisfied the other side because of our solicitor's word. We would be late and as per the contract they could have taken our deposit and remarketed the property. Our solicitor did this because we had such a good relationship with her, because we'd done so many transactions with her in the past. The fundamental reason why, and I didn't know this at this stage, this investor failed to perform is that they were waiting on releasing funds from another project through re-mortgage. Going that close to the wire, over-promising, often causes unnecessary stress. The investor was subject to extra stress and it's not something I would have chosen to do had I known. However, we'd made it. We had purchased the property.

Simultaneously, we submitted detailed planning applications for the fifteen flats that we'd been told would not be a problem. More on that now.

Part Three: Planning

If you've just finished the last section, you'll know that after a few hairy moments, we got the funds in place and we purchased the Paradigm property for £323,500. We had been assured by the planners and the mayor that we wouldn't have any issues with this project. We had now submitted the detailed planning application for fifteen flats, which is what we said we were going to do all along. It all seemed to be going pretty well for a week or two and then a conservation officer got involved. He needed to because this was a Grade II listed building, and of course as soon as you start doing things with a Grade II listed building, you're going to get the conservation officer involved. There were no alarm bells ringing at this point in time.

Then we started receiving a few phone calls and messages from our architect and it became obvious that all was not well. If you recall from earlier on in this chapter, to get the full fifteen flats in there was a requirement to remove the third staircase that was a late addition and had no historical value. The conservation officer was insistent that this third staircase remain.

Now, if that were the case, our architect told us that the absolute best he could do, because staircases by their very nature take up quite a lot of space, was to give us a revised proposal with thirteen flats, albeit some of the flats were obviously going to be slightly larger. Adding back the space that was required for the staircase, it wasn't possible in any way shape or form to come up with a sensible plan for fifteen flats. We took advice on this and we wrote to the council. The council apologised. The message was effectively, 'we're really sorry, we gave you the best information we had at the time.' There were clear signs of embarrassment all round, but ultimately it wasn't possible to get the proposal for fifteen through. So, having taken advice, the proposal that actually went to the Planning Committee was a proposal for thirteen flats.

The conservation officer wasn't finished yet. He was completely insistent on every small point of every piece of coving, woodwork and skirting board. By the time it got to the Planning Committee, he wasn't prepared to support even the proposal for thirteen flats, so the planners themselves came to us with a suggested compromise. They said, 'Okay, we've talked to our colleagues in conservation and we believe we can get them to support a proposal for eleven flats.' Just before we started shouting and screaming, they said, 'But, we have a thought for you to get extra GDV...'

In the grounds of Paradigm there were some outbuildings, a mixture of garages and storage units that adjoined a pub next door, a very nice pub indeed. Their proposal was that we submit an application, and I must emphasise that they told us to submit the application, for either one big bungalow or two semi-detached bungalows that could be formed from a combination of knocking down some of the outbuildings and building onto the footprint of where those outbuildings currently were. The planners were clearly embarrassed and said they would absolutely support an additional planning application for one or two bungalows.

So, having gone from fifteen to thirteen, we were now more or less being told to go from thirteen to eleven flats with the planners saying that whether they supported it or not (which meant they didn't want to) they were convinced the conservation officer would torpedo planning even if they tried to steer it through. This was a long way from the original plan. The original plan had been fifteen in the original building and as a second stage development we had thoughts along the lines that we might develop other areas of the site, but the core of the project was fifteen flats in the main house.

That had been eroded down to thirteen flats with the blame being put on the conservation officer. By now it was just eleven flats. Fifteen down to eleven is a huge erosion in margin, but it was also compounded by the return our investors expected. When we believed we had fifteen flats, we'd been prepared to offer the two quarter of a million pound investors one flat as a return. This would have been one fifteenth of the GDV each. Two fifteenths would have been the total costs for their half million pound investment. This had now jumped up to two elevenths.

Of course, the council had no way of knowing this, and I'm not saying this was in any way, shape or form the council's fault. The way the deal was built was that two of our investors would take one flat each and now the GDV was shrinking all the time from fifteen to thirteen to eleven flats. The cost of the finance was therefore ratcheting in the opposite direction, because the fraction of that GDV that their one flat represented was getting bigger and bigger.

Our architect gave us assurances that the best way to deal with the council was to be collaborative and cooperative and he offered to draw up proposals for the two bungalows at a nominal rate. With huge reluctance we re-submitted the plans to the Planning Committee. The GDV didn't look too bad although it was nowhere near the fifteen flat scenario, but versus the thirteen flats, eleven flats and two semi-detached bungalows should mean we were not going to be too much out of pocket. It was not as good as planned, but it wasn't that bad.

And now, enter stage left yet another conservation officer! This time not a listed building conservation officer but a tree conservation officer. The gardens at the back of the property verged on parkland and I don't want to make it sound too grand, but there's around three quarters of an acre at the back of Paradigm. This is in addition to the grounds that belong to Paradigm, which are mainly laid to tarmac for a car park. There is a small grassy area that included some trees and here was the issue. There was a nice large tree in Paradigm's back garden. This tree wasn't going to be disturbed by the proposed bungalows, but some of the tree's branches would have overhung one of the bungalow's roof.

The tree conservation officer's position was not that we were going to chop the tree down or cause any direct damage to the tree. His position was that this deciduous tree (sorry to go all biological on you here, but that means it drops its leaves every winter i.e. it's not an evergreen) was going to keep dropping all its leaves into the bungalow's gutters. He felt that over time the owner would get irritated by the leaves and start lopping branches off to stop the tree dropping leaves into the gutters. The statement was that even if we did not do this, future owners or future inhabitants of these bungalows would. So never mind, 'guilty until proven innocent,' sorry, 'innocent until proven guilty' (or did I get that right the first time?), this was a projected, possible, future event against a tree that wasn't listed, and it was stopping the development of the two bungalows.

Now, if this is where the planning process in the UK has got to, if this is how councils are going to treat developers, I will be nothing short of amazed if anything ever happens to fundamentally change the nature of the massive UK housing crisis that we're in. The system would rather protect unlisted tree branches from potential damage than provide homes. I found this whole episode amazing. I have been through planning many times and I have never, ever seen anything like this before or since.

There's no shortage of people wanting to build houses and it would also appear there's no shortage of council officials wanting to stop them. We had assurances at the very highest level that we could have fifteen flats. Then it was thirteen flats and then 'we're really sorry.' Then it was 'Oh my God, we're very truly sorry but it is going to have to be eleven flats,' but you can have two bungalows instead. One of their own staff then appears and says, 'No, bungalows not allowed, you can't do that.'

Yet more apologetic phone calls from the planners to say there's no way we're going to get this through. There's no way to get the tree conservation officer on side. It had looked like a very attractive project with fifteen flats plus future development potential in the grounds, but we were now effectively being told, by the very same people, sorry we got that wrong: it will be eleven flats and no future development potential in the grounds. Paradigm had become a very, very different proposition.

Our specialists, our architect and our quantity surveyor, told us we really had no options. The planning was re-submitted for a third time, at yet more cost and fees, and this time planning was approved. The GDV had now shrunk dramatically because there were so many fewer flats, and of course, as previously mentioned, according to the agreement that the LLP had struck with the investors, two of these flats would need to be given away.

So effectively, we needed to balance the books on the GDV of nine of the flats, accepting the fact that the LLP would need to pay for all eleven of the flats to be developed. This was very far short of a good combination of events.

In the future would I ever do a Grade II listed building conversion again without prior detailed planning being given? I'd certainly have to think long and hard. Here is the challenge. Once planning is approved, then planning gain is factored into the purchase cost. It gets much more expensive to buy. It is sometimes possible to buy subject to planning, but the vendors were not allowing this option. If I did a similar project again it would need to be using 'stress-free' money.

What is stress-free money? Stress-free money is simply this: money that is not subject to any requirement to earn interest for anybody, anytime in the next three to four years. If it can be a genuine speculative 'punt' then no problem. Paradigm wasn't. This was 'stressed money' and more of that later on in this chapter. The investors needed a return on their funds. We later discovered two of the three investors could not afford to leave their money invested for an unspecified period. They needed results.

We now had planning, albeit not what we wanted. In this next section of this chapter, we're going to move on to next steps.

Next Steps

Having got the planning, we now needed to satisfy the requirements of building control. Now in case you're reading this in Scotland, just to translate, that's building warrants. With a listed building in England obtaining the building control is far more like obtaining building warrants in Scotland for this simple reason: you would have to be crazy to start without full building control approval as you are likely to have to start again or even pay fines. You need to have confirmed detailed specification which the council has agreed is appropriate and which will meet noise requirements, thermal insulation and any other tests that they might want to put against it, for example acoustic installation.

Normally in England and Wales the project can just start with the anticipation that building control will sign it off in the future. That does not happen in Scotland and neither does it happen in England for listed buildings.

So yet again we needed the historical conservation officer to come and talk to us about the ins and outs of different building materials and the specifics of what each room would look like from an aesthetic point of view. Room by room, square foot by square foot, we had to have a detailed discussion about what we had to preserve. The architect, the quantity surveyor and the conservation officer went around and literally marked-up doors, walls, architrave and plasterwork. There were detailed notes and markings all over that property. All of this had to be integrated into the drawings. The architect's pack was now many hundreds of pages, pictures and CDs.

Once this was finalised (which took months), we started to get detailed costings to do the development. In order to do that we had needed this level of detail from all the professionals. I could just see the costs rising pen-stroke by pen-stroke, professional fee by professional fee.

We were building a full-scale tender document. The process is very different when spending an estimated £600,000 on detailed building work. It is not a question of phoning three local builders for a quote! We needed a full tender document and the tender went to multiple main contractors, all of whom were directed that we would use a JCT contract. A project this size is going to need to be controlled by architects, quantity surveyors and the other professionals. Not one of us popping round after work on a Friday evening just to check everything was all right. It needed a detailed level of supervision.

By the time the conservation officer had finished with us, and the architect, the tender document was over 2,000 pages including addendums, drawings and detailed specifications. It was a terrifying thing to look at. It occupied ring binders, it had CDs accompanying it, all sorts of levels of detail. This tender document went out to ten different companies who were judged to be financially stable enough and reputable enough to be able to pull off a project of this stature.

This was in October 2015, following the purchase in the July 2015. It had taken us that long to get the specification agreed. Four months. The deadline for return of tender documents was the following December. Of the ten companies, five indicated they didn't have the resources to prepare a tender. It was simply going to be too much work for them to even put together a quote. Of the other five contractors that said they would, only one actually returned the tender to the deadline.

This is another lesson. Earlier in this chapter I said that there is a sweet spot for projects between one and four million, and there genuinely is. But there's a major caveat to this: you need strong relationships with builders to take advantage of this. One million to four million is not a sweet spot for main contractors. Project spends of a million or less don't really carry enough margin to make it interesting for a main contractor. It's way above the resources of a self-employed single builder but way below the resources and infrastructure that's set up to support big construction projects. So, it's a specialist area where, with the requisite project management skills and connections, it can be very attractive.

You almost become the main contractor and then directly employ various sub-contractors on a shell and core basis. In other words, one or two sub-contractors to make the envelope, the walls, the roof and the windows secure. Then another couple of contractors working on the core of the building. To have a main contractor looking after the whole thing is probably going to cost at least fifteen per cent on top of all of the sub-contractors' quotes.

Given the lack of response to tenders, we extended the deadline to the end of January. By the end of January 2016, we were in receipt of four quotes. The architect and the quantity surveyor went through the quotes and we were presented with the preferred quote. Against an original budget of £590,000, the preferred quote was £1.8 million! Three times the original cost estimate and clearly completely untenable. Not only was this a budgetary development sum that we found difficult to comprehend, it would have taken away almost one hundred per cent of the GDV on its own.

With the new plans, we had the estate agents back to give us estimates for the GDV based on the 11 flats. The highest of these estimates was £2.4 million and the lowest of which was £1.2 million. As it was such a huge spread, we paid for a RICS (Royal Institute of Chartered Surveyors) commercial surveyor to give us a RICS GDV. This was assessed at £2,130,000.

Even if we accepted the RICS GDV of £2.1 million, it was going to make absolutely no sense whatsoever to spend £1.8 million in order to achieve that. We'd already spent £335,000 to acquire the building and by this time well in excess of £80,000 on professional fees. Planning, architects, surveyors, quantity surveyors, intrusive surveys and works that needed to be done to satisfy the conservation officer. The costs just kept on mounting up.

It is important to note that over this period the four partners in the LLP, myself, Aniko and the two local partners, had not received one single penny in compensation. All of this work, all of these phone calls, all of these visits, everything that we were doing was completely and absolutely in anticipation of potential future profits.

What Next?

Okay, I'm an engineer. I am very used to large construction projects. Over the years I've supervised the building of factories, distilleries, warehouses and much more. It had not been on my agenda to do what I did next, but my skillset allowed me to do it. I went into the operational project team to do some cost and value engineering with the main suppliers. Coming out of that process, we managed to agree a reduced scope of work at a reduced specification which didn't contravene any of the conservation officer's requirements. We got one of the four main contractors to revise their proposed quotation down to £1.3 million and then with some further scope revision and negotiation, finally to £1 million. However, this did not include any contingency.

We now just about had a potentially viable project. £1 million of development plus £415,000 of purchase costs and professional fees plus contingency would give us a total spend of £1.5 million. GDV was forecast in the range of £1.2m to £2.4m from the estate agents. As previously mentioned, we therefore made the decision to pay for a full RICS development appraisal which came back fully documented at £2.1 million, so the view could be taken that £1.8 million was a slightly conservative GDV expectation some £300,000 below RICS.

There were also two additional sources of value for the project.
Firstly, the freehold. We were creating eleven new leaseholds for the flats. Typically, a freehold will sell for perhaps twenty to twenty-two times the

income received from the leaseholders. So, if we set the ground rents in the lease at a few hundred pounds each per year, then times eleven flats, this might take annual ground rent income to say £3,000. Times this by twenty-two for the freehold sale multiplier and this might take us to £66,000 or perhaps even £70,000. There was some value there. Freeholds are seen as extremely safe long-term (low yield) investments and there is a ready market for this kind of deal. Of course, freehold sale was not the reason we did the Paradigm project, but equally why not take the value that is there?

Second were the capital allowances. I have covered capital allowances in other places, but as a quick reminder this is income that can be earned tax free by the legal entity owning the property. These have value in themselves. The capital allowances would be very significant, hundreds of thousands of pounds, when this project was complete. Depending on final project spend and materials used, a sensible estimate is £300,000 of capital allowances on this project. If these were then claimed by a forty per cent tax payer, that would be worth another £120,000. If £300,000 is earned tax-fee and tax is at forty per cent, the tax saving is £120,000. It is not income, it is a tax saving. In order for someone to claim their share of tax savings they would need to have been a partner in the LLP. How the value would be extracted would depend on the final structure. In summary, £60,000 to £70,000 for the freehold sale and £120,000 or so in value from capital allowances. Roughly an extra £200,000 not factored into the RICS valuation.

Armed with all this information, we went back to the investors and said look, this isn't what we planned, but here are the numbers. How can we work our way through this? This was the first time the investors, rather than behaving as three of our friends, colleagues and partners, started behaving as investors who wanted their return.

Their message back to us (and I'm paraphrasing) was: 'The erosion of margin is a risk to the developer rather than the investors.' I'm not criticising that, it was their choice and furthermore it was their decision to elect a spokesperson. So, rather than dealing with three investors, we were now dealing with one investors' representative. Again, no criticism of their decision but it did have consequences later on.

Here is the overview of the changes to Project Paradigm versus original assumptions.

With an original estimated build cost, paid for from a professional quantity surveyor of £590,000, a purchase cost of £335,000 and £75,000 worth of professional fees had planning gone smoothly first time, instead of the third time, we would have been looking at a total cost of £1 million for fifteen flats. This was the number that quite often featured in our early discussions. As I've said previously, with £800,000 of private finance, that kind of build could be managed with some off-plan sales, building of some show homes and phasing the development with no additional outside input of funds.

You may be wondering (as we did!) how the quantity surveyor got it so wrong. To give one specific example, the property has wooden sash windows and internal shutters. The conservation officer insisted we had to repair (i.e. not replace) all the windows and shutters using original materials. The lowest quote through the tender we identified for this single element was in excess of £84,000. Wildly higher than replacement costs.
Here is a table of the revised financials for just eleven versus the original fifteen apartments:

Here is a table of the revised financials for just eleven versus the original fifteen apartments:

	Original Assumptions	Revised Assumptions
Acquisition costs including stamp duty	£335,000	£335,000
Build costs including contingency	£590,000	£1,100,000
Various professional fees	£75,000	£165,000
TOTAL COST ESTIMATES	£1.000.000	£1,600,000
Valuation range	£1.8m - £3.0m	£1.2m - £2.4m (RICS £2.1m)
Private finance	£800,000 (pledged)	£609,500 (released)
Freehold plus Capital Allowances	£180,000	£180,000

With a £1 million build cost, to which we added a ten per cent contingency, plus £400,000 of spend so far, we were looking at between £1.5 and £1.6 million total costs. This was a total of sixty per cent escalation in costs. At the same time, there had been a de-escalation or a compression of GDV due to the fact that we could now only get eleven units instead of fifteen. Added to the mix was the fact that we received £609,500 in private funds and not the full £800,000 pledged from the investor group. It was now absolutely clear that we were going to need a substantial third party, bank or bridging lending.

This, of course, carries other implications. We had this conversation with our investors and their position was, again paraphrasing, 'If you need to borrow money, go and borrow money, however we still expect our return.' Aniko and I started conversations with our commercial broker and very quickly we found parties that were prepared to lend. Now what did that mean? It meant that the project was still salvageable. With a spend of £1.6 million, a GDV mid-range of £1.8 to £2.1m, plus £60,000 for the freehold and £120,000 for capital allowances, the project was still viable but becoming marginal.

For a lender to advance £1 million to allow the next stage of Paradigm was possible, but it wasn't the cheapest option. We were looking at interest rates in the range of eight to nine per cent for eighteen months. This would add another £150,000 of cost to the project.
Then we had to factor in the arrangement with the first two investors to give them a flat each and pay the third investor interest whether Paradigm breaks even or loses money. 9 elevenths of the GDV of £2.1million, minus investor interest, minus bank interest, plus freehold value, plus capital allowances would allow us to break even at best. We needed to renegotiate terms with the investors if this was going to work.

In our view, the best thing to do was bite the bullet, develop it out, get the project finished and return to the investors as much as possible and minimise the damage. Not every investment is going to make you a multi-millionaire. Some investments are going to give you hard lessons. You've heard me use the phrase before, 'if you're not earning, you're learning.' We certainly did some learning on this project! One of the key things we were learning was investor management and the ten per cent rule. I'll come back to the ten per cent rule later.

The investor group, from our perspective, and I can well appreciate they'll have their own perspective, was becoming increasingly intransigent. 'Do what you need to do, it's your responsibility, we want the return that we were promised.' Promise is a strong word. Even if you use a word like 'commitment', that was in the context of a specific set of numbers. If those numbers change, in the business world, the deal needs to change. The less flexibility you've got from your investor group, the less options you have. Again, I repeat, this is not a criticism, it's just an observation.

Armed with the offer of finance, I went to the investor group on behalf of the LLP to let them know we had the finance secured. This was in March 2016. In order to take advantage of this finance, the investors would need to release their charges because the investor coming in, a bank in this case, is simply not going to release £1 million unless they've got first charge. Unfortunately, this was not acceptable to the current investor group. This stunned me. At this point, I really didn't know what to do next. In our experience you could not expect a financial institution to offer a significant loan, £1 million, without first charge security on the project.

Here is a universal law: banks or bridging companies will not embark on a project without the funds in place to build it out. If you disappear, if your organisation disappears, your company or LLP disappears, for them to be left with a half-finished building site that's perhaps consumed eighty per cent of the funds is of no value whatsoever. They want to know they can go in and finish the job, taking over from you, without the need for any additional funds or resources. That requires first charge on the project and the release of the funds in staged payments against sign off by an independent quantity surveyor that they will typically supply or an architect, again that they will supply. We were now in a position where we couldn't get lending without the release of securities, which meant we couldn't complete the project.

As you can imagine, there were many discussions to find a mutually beneficial solution, but we were struggling to find one. Paraphrasing the investor group's position, they said, 'You personally, Paul, were the reason that we invested in this project. We know you're a man of means, we know that you earn significant money, do it from your own funds.'

Here's another fundamental rule of business: just because you can, doesn't mean you should. The fundamental disconnect between the LLP and the investor group meant that their perception was Paradigm was 'Paul's project.' We used solicitors to draw up the agreement, so everybody was aware that the legal entity they'd contracted with was an LLP with four partners at the start. It was not Paul personally.

We had many correspondences along the lines that other than the funds they'd injected, which in two of the investors' cases was less than they'd promised, were invested in the LLP. The LLP had the building, it had some cash, it had planning permission, but that's all it had. If they were not prepared to release security, the only thing I could suggest was we would liquidate the LLP, sell the property with planning permission and hopefully enjoy some planning gain.

The bank finance offer had now lapsed.

Our two local partners in Doncaster had had enough by this stage. It had been endless amounts of work, what they perceived to be lack of support from our investors and no real prospect of reward, so they both resigned from the LLP. Somewhat ironically, the two partners who had the local knowledge and were managing the project, left us metaphorically 'holding the baby' together with our unhappy investors. We don't like letting people down, so we kept looking for solutions.

Although relations were strained, there was still a level of cordiality. We were still trying to get the project to work. We were looking for other investors, private funds, people to take the whole thing over. Obviously if people had that kind of liquidity, if they had £1-1.5 million, they wouldn't need to charge the project funding costs. There were other people out there in the universe who could have done this project for less. Maybe they were main contractors themselves. If the main contractor margin at the £1.1 million development cost was £150,000-£200,000, plus if they had the liquidity, then there would be no finance costs. They could potentially do the project for as much as £300,000 to £350,000 less than the LLP could.

So, it wasn't all doom and gloom, there was still some positivity. Let's get this done. We all wanted to get it done and get it behind us. This project was now moving to its resolution phase.

Part Four: Resolution

We wanted to get Paradigm funded. By now, you're familiar with the numbers. You know that the number of flats had reduced from fifteen to thirteen to eleven. You also know that the build costs went from £590,000 to £1.1 million.

You also know that we had a funding requirement. It made no sense to go back and ask for funding on the same basis the investors had already rejected, so we needed to come up with something different if we were going to have any chance of making this work.

The LLP approached the investor group on this basis and sought to renegotiate the terms of the borrowing, the terms of the investment from them. They now knew that there weren't many routes left and they actively engaged in this discussion. The LLP paid their legal fees for them to be advised and new documentation was drawn up to replace the original loan agreements. These loan agreements said that for the first two charge investors, they would retain their first charge for now, but instead of receiving a flat as compensation, which was destroying the margin for the project given the new situation, that they would receive interest. For all three of the investors, as well as receiving interest and their principal being repaid over time, the LLP, as far as it was able, would start making regular, monthly payments. These documents were all signed, and the monthly payments started in November 2016.

Now clearly, the LLP could only make these payments whilst it had money if it was to do anything other than simply return to them the balance of their funds. It needed to start earning money, dispose the project and do something to generate value, such that the LLP had the resources to fulfil its obligations. On the positive side, we at least now had investor contracts that were less onerous and the margins, therefore, were likely to be better for the project.

With the new agreement in place, we began demolition at the property and preparatory works. We employed the preferred contractor and the strip out began. By March 2017 we had secured another finance offer for construction funding to build out the project.

The new lender required first charge with no other charges on the property. The building in its existing state was valued at £300,000, given strip out had already started, utilities were disconnected, and the place was a building site. We proposed paying a total of £150,000 to the investors collectively when releasing their charges whilst accepting the construction funding at the same time. We also offered £150,000 personal guarantees. The build was estimated to take ten to twelve months.

Once the building was finished, the LLP would then re-finance and aim to pay to the investors the balance owed to them at that point. If there was a shortfall the LLP would make good any shortfall from its monthly income using the units as high-end serviced accommodation. It would have productive assets as opposed to a pile of stone costing money to insure and secure.

Unfortunately, this offer was again rejected by the investors.

By this time, we, as partners of the LLP, had injected £75,000 of our own funds to pay the investors monthly and to pay for the security of the building, insurance and ongoing legal fees. The LLP had literally no other resources.

The lender was asking for an £800,000 personal guarantee. If the deal went ahead we would be giving the investors £150,000 of personal guarantees and we would also return £150,000 cash back to the investors. In total, this was either cash or personal guarantees, from our perspective, of £1.2 million. The investors responded through their spokesperson: 'No.'

I was the most surprised and disappointed that I've probably ever been in my professional life.

We just wanted to get the project started so the building could be finished and start earning money, instead of the never-ending expenses. We were back to the drawing board once again.

We decided to make one final attempt to find a solution by turning Paradigm into an office and training space for another one of our companies. With our broker's help, a mainstream bank became involved. Given Paradigm was already an office, to refurbish it as an office would require much less funds and would be easier with regards to permissions, although the end value would also be less. We put a deal together that would allow us to satisfy the investors latest requirements.

The time that had elapsed since the start of the project seemed like a lifetime. In reality, it was less than two years. So much had happened in those two years.

I took great care and much thought before making our final offer. Because that is exactly what it was. A final offer. This really was the end of the road. It was taking up massive amounts of our time. We felt there was nowhere to go after that. So, if the investors didn't like this, they better come up with an idea of their own.

In order to support the bank lending, NatWest were again looking for significant personal guarantees from Aniko and myself. We were the last two remaining partners in the LLP, just to remind you, our two previous partners had resigned and left.

We obtained construction quotes to turn the building into an office and training space. Within weeks we obtained an offer of funding in principle, subject to significant amount of details, but things started to look positive again. Yet again, we started a seemingly endless administrative job to complete forms, meet the bankers and satisfy the various requirements from the bank. The investors, in the meantime, wanted deadlines for completion whilst the bank was asking for more and more information.

The next communication we had was that the investors had decided to repossess. We told the investors, 'There's no need to repossess, we will happily give you the keys and sign it over.' We had no use for the asset as we would not be able to finalise finance now that the repossession had started. It was now impossible for the project to proceed, why would we want to keep hold of the asset?

As you can imagine, emotions were high. There were selective 'leaks' and people in social media exchanges judged me and my performance in the complete absence of ever having spoken to me or having any knowledge of the details of the project. I have maintained almost complete public silence on this project until now. Aniko and I, on behalf of the LLP, but also on behalf of ourselves as individuals, chose to keep our own council.

Our other trading businesses started to suffer from the unfounded social media attacks. Contracts were cancelled, speaking engagements were cancelled. It's difficult to put a precise figure on it in terms of financial loss to our other businesses, but it will be comfortably in the several hundred thousand plus range.

As Dr John Demartini always says: 'There can never only be a downside. Every one of us is subject to equal measures of support and challenge. The harder you are challenged, the more support you will get.' So, for all that there were people very openly attacking me, there were others on a personal basis, that were being incredibly supportive.

We had formed Touchstone Education by this time and we decided to go fully independent as wealth and property education providers. It has been the best thing we ever did. I'm not sure we ever would have done it without Project Paradigm and the challenges it brought with it. Whatever doesn't kill you, makes you stronger. That is certainly true, my friends, in all walks of life. Personal, business and financial. Whatever doesn't kill you, makes you stronger.

The attacks got to such a point that we felt, not from a personal point of view but from a reputational damage point of view for our companies, that we no longer wished to suffer them. We employed a respected London law firm to defend ourselves. They acted on our behalf and found that almost all the attacks were foundation-less and opinion-based. Most of this has now been removed from social media. There are still clearly people out there, in social media land, 'the haters', that don't feel that their judgement has been executed.

It's inevitably true that the more successful you become, the more haters you attract. The person that writes better about haters than anyone else, in my experience, is Grant Cardone. He revels in the fact that he's got haters. So, I suppose, I should take it as a badge of honour that I've got some. I don't think I've got as many as him (yet!). He thinks it's a good thing if you've got haters. If nobody hates you, then you don't stand for anything. If nobody hates you, nobody's ever heard of you.

So, How Did This Project End?

We went through the process that the investors wanted us to go through. The property eventually went to auction and was sold in December 2017 which ended the project.

It could have been so different, and in the final part of this chapter, I'm going to focus on what lessons we've learned. What we'd do differently and what we already do differently now. I want to talk about the ten per cent rule too. I want to talk about how you could potentially take these lessons and make sure you learn vicariously through our experiences, so you never have an experience like this.

I hope you're enjoying this book so far. I know I've taken you on a long journey, everywhere from my childhood, under the floors of Victorian properties in Yorkshire, through Essex, Newcastle, London, and back again to Yorkshire, where it all began. My love of business, my love of finance and my love of property has remained undiminished. My learnings inform the way that I approach the various projects that I get involved in, the people that I deal with and the structures that I put in place.

As well as the lessons, I want to look at what could have happened and what could have been done to me personally, if I hadn't taken some of the precautions that I took.

Part Five: Lessons Learned

This has been a big chapter with lots of learnings, and what I want to focus on now is precisely that. Learnings. What could, or would we do differently?

If we review the various stages of the process, the Paradigm project, the first was obviously becoming aware of the project. As Napoleon Hill says, the process is 'conceive, believe, achieve.' We can't possibly do something unless we've got a concept that something might be possible.

So, the concept, the idea that perhaps we could do something with Paradigm, clearly originated when it first came to our attention that Paradigm was available. Okay, now here in itself is the first lesson, because it was opportunistic. It wasn't informed by strategy. It wasn't a specific type of property strategy in a specific area. It was just, 'oh this looks good, we could do this.' So, it's not something that we had a specific expertise in. Yes, we were property specialists, but we weren't Grade II, listed building commercial conversion specialists in Doncaster. Know your area, know your strategy and stick to it.

There's a heck of a difference between having a general knowledge of many different property strategies and being very clear about what your property strategies are. Many of you will have heard of the '80/20 rule', the Pareto Principle. It's clearly the case that most of the projects are not going to be suitable for most of the people. Most property projects are not going to be suitable for most property people. So be very clear about your area, be very clear about your strategy, and be very clear about the projects that you get involved in. Paradigm, with hindsight, was fundamentally a distraction, because it was not a core competence for us. That's the first lesson.

Number two. Whilst Aniko and I could, I'm sure, have done this project, (if we weren't doing everything else) we were doing so many other things, that we were expecting our local partners to do far more than they did. I'm not going to start blaming a relatively young joint venture partner. He was full of energy and he brought lots to the table. I guess my surprise was that I assumed, and you know what they say about assumption, the experience level of his uncle. We incorrectly judged the level of capability he would bring to the project. You will occasionally find a project that is 'so good' you want to try and do it, even though it's not necessarily something you've ever done before. If you don't try something new, you will never do anything different. However, the second lesson is that if you do get taken off course, if you do go off-track, and I assure you that you will get the opportunity, please, please, please make sure that you've got a fantastically strong team with expertise to support you in that endeavour, and critically, be very clear about individual accountabilities. I'm not saying for one minute that we were reckless and that we shouldn't have done it. All I am saying is that in retrospect, it was not a core project in a priority area covered by one of our core competencies.

To summarise these first two learnings: you'll often make more money by saying NO than by saying YES to everything. In fact, if you're saying yes to everything, you're definitely going to come a cropper at some point because nobody can do everything, every project in every area.

We were living in Scotland and Paradigm was many hours' drive from our home. It was in our 'goldmine area' but it was our goldmine area for HMOs, not commercial conversions, especially Grade II listed commercial conversions. If you are going to go 'off-piste', because as I've said there will perhaps be that temptation to mine some new extra gold, well, make one hundred per cent sure that your team is fantastically strong.

Next, when we were doing the feasibility stage for this project we engaged with professionals. I'm not blaming those professionals, I'm just observing. We paid many, many thousands of pounds, in fact many tens of thousands of pounds, to these professionals. I'm talking about architects, quantity surveyors, and other specialists. Despite investing all of that, our build cost estimates turned out to be almost one hundred per cent too low. Actual build costs almost doubled versus estimates. In fact, some of the individual quote elements more than trebled from the original build estimates. That's obviously a huge variance. Furthermore, despite our architect's best efforts, liaison with the council at the very highest level and the assurances we had received, our expectation of getting fifteen units resulted in us getting permission, eventually, for just eleven. This was a huge variance. Now, what could we have done about that in retrospect? I'm not sure we could have done very much. All the professionals we engaged were just that, professionals, with a good local reputation. It wasn't like we were pulling in professionals from miles away or even the wrong country, as I've seen done before. These were actually professionals living and working in that local market.

Could we have spent yet more money and taken second opinions? I guess we could. Could we have doubled all the estimates they gave us? Well, I guess we could. But for me, the lesson here is we did as much due diligence as could possibly have been expected in any normal scenario with such a business case in front of us. We just have to accept the fact that sometimes due diligence is not infallible. We have to accept the fact that even with the professionals involved it can go horribly wrong. Ultimately, that's why it's called 'property investing.' It's not called 'Property Guaranteed Profit.'

With every investment, there's a risk. Risk and reward are, the free market says, a balance. So typically, the higher the reward, the higher the risk. Do all the due diligence that you reasonably can in order to minimise that risk. Also do everything you can to boost the reward, but the fact remains, risk and reward are linked.

Next, let's look at the way in which our relationship ultimately deteriorated with our investors. It was not something that any of us would have wanted to happen. I'm sure the investors themselves would not have wanted it to happen. I've already given indications along the way of what perhaps could have been done differently.
Here's where I want to talk about the ten per cent rule. All of us, as human beings, are tolerant to variances of ten per cent.

Imagine that you have a portfolio of stocks and shares and imagine that that portfolio's valued at £100,000. You do an annual review. I'm going give you a few different scenarios. Scenario one: that portfolio of stocks and shares has grown by six per cent. It's okay, it's kind of what you expected it to do. The long-term average return from the stock market is seven per cent, so six per cent is in line with expectations. It's a little tiny bit lower than you might have expected, but ultimately, you're not going to go and change your investment strategy because you're one per cent adrift of your expectations. Neither are you going to start running about telling everyone that you are now, in fact, Warren Buffet reincarnate. It's a normal return. So, you'll probably carry on, you may review your portfolio, you might think about perhaps using a different adviser, but ultimately nothing much changes because you're tolerant to plus or minus ten per cent versus your expectations on return.

Let's take that same scenario and over the same year, the same portfolio of stocks and shares has had a different outcome. Instead of being worth £100,000, it's now worth £77,000. Your heart is probably going to be in your mouth, stomach, wherever it is when you're upset. You are going to start panicking. £100,000 is important to you and it's just gone down by twenty-three per cent when you expected it to go up by seven per cent. That is wildly outside your expectations and you're going to do all kinds of irrational things. Maybe you'll sell your portfolio, fire your adviser or look for a different adviser. Maybe you're going get out of stocks and shares all together. 'I knew stocks and shares didn't work,' you will tell everyone that will listen. 'Sounded too good to be true, it obviously is. I'm not doing stocks and shares any more, it's a disaster.'

Under normal, rational circumstances everybody knows that stocks and shares do work over the (very) long-term. As it says on every advert for this I've ever seen, 'the value of investment may go up as well as down.' You don't think about it as average, you think, 'Jesus, I can't be affording to lose this kind of money. This is going kill me,' because it's outside of your ten per cent tolerance.

Now conversely, on the upside, let's say that this same portfolio of stocks and shares in a different year has actually made thirty-two per cent and it's gone from £100,000, because it will (sometimes), to £132,000. Wow. There's nothing anymore that anybody can teach you about the stock market. You are now the expert. You can go and borrow money off people for 'just 8%.' You can invest it in the stock market and you can pick up the other twenty-four per cent because you know how to make thirty-two per cent per annum, you just did it. Every time you go out for a drink or go to a dinner party, you lecture people on the need to get into stocks and shares, because they 'can't afford not to, this market isn't going to last forever.' They need to be working with someone like you!

Do you see what I'm saying? We're all tolerant to plus or minus ten per cent. So, here's the learning and here's very much what we do now. We do far fewer joint ventures, although that's a separate point that I'll come to shortly. For the joint ventures we do, we will not work with more than ten percent of someone's disposable wealth. Now, what's their disposable wealth? Essentially, it's something they don't live in, i.e. it's not their home and it's not something that's part of their pension plan. It's cash that sits outside of what they need to live in or what they're intending to live from in their golden years.

Now think what that does to the attitude of the investor. Suddenly, it's an amount of money that they can afford to lose, they can afford to risk it because investment means exactly that. There's an expectation of a return, but there's also a risk. Now, imagine that I'd been working with three investors that had many millions of pounds. When things started to go wrong, they could have fixed it fairly easily at the stroke of a pen by investing more. They would have been far more likely to release their charges to allow the project to progress if they were only risking ten per cent of their disposable wealth. It would have taken away a lot of financial pressure. More importantly, it wouldn't have mattered to them to the same extent. If they were top rate tax payers and they could write off their investment against tax as a loss, well, they're only actually losing forty-seven per cent of the money invested. The highest rate of tax in the UK is forty-five per cent. The true rate of tax at forty-five per cent is actually fifty-three per cent by the time you add on national insurance. The attitude of this group of HNW (High Net Worth) people is wildly different to normal people. They perhaps think, 'I've punted a million quid this year, if thirty-three per cent of it does really well and triples in value, well that's all my money back. The rest of it I can just write off against tax. I'd rather invest it in speculative projects than pay the tax.'

I'm not saying you have to work with super-rich people. I am saying that whenever you choose to joint venture with someone and they're investing their capital, make sure it's not more than ten per cent of their disposable wealth. Otherwise, if challenges arise there's likely to be a major breakdown in communications as they are overwhelmed by fear of loss and no longer act rationally. That's the ten per cent rule. I hope you find it useful.

The ten per cent rule alone would have saved a lot of heartache on this project because, very simply, it would not have happened. Let's move on to some of the other points.

Let's focus on the architect, in particular. We'd received assurances about planning and that's why we submitted planning in the first instance for fifteen flats. I've gone through it, and I'm not going to go through it again, but despite assurances of the very highest level from the council, that's not what was delivered. Whenever you're dealing with a council, and this isn't a dig at people that have or are giving their lives to the service of the public in various roles, it's just a fact: they are not as heavily invested in your project as you are. So, they may say one thing and do another. You have to expect that. In hindsight, I'd rather have walked away from this deal and lost it than the scenario that we ended up with. What do I mean specifically? I now know that we should have got the planning first, before we purchased the property. Many people don't think that's possible because as soon as the owner, or other people, see planning applications go in, that drives up the value of the property. Consider taking an option on the building or take a lockout agreement. We have done this before, so why didn't we do it in this case?

I had never been in an environment before where the planners, the architects and the mayoress herself were all saying, 'We're going to make sure that you get the right support on this.' I put too much credence in, let's call them, 'assurances.' I'm not blaming anyone except myself for this, but I took too much on good faith, and that's the first point. Our partners in the LLP were pushing strongly and our investors wanted to do the project so there were many people urging us on.

Secondly, I'm a competitive person and there was a lot of peer pressure. I knew other people in our mentorship club that were doing big deals. The competitive part of me was saying, 'Well, I've got to find a big project somewhere. Otherwise, I'm going to be a failure compared to others. And I don't want that.' So, I did something I probably wouldn't normally have done, given a different environment and competitive set. Now I know not everybody will have that in their make up, but if you do, please be aware of it, please make sure you get somebody to help you see the risks you might potentially be taking.

Another lesson we learned is this: write out a list of all the upsides for the project, get them all documented. Perhaps it would be a great service to the community, to get a gorgeous, old, but very run-down building back into use. Literally write this down and keep going until you've got a minimum of twenty, ideally fifty, plus points, all upsides.

Now, set yourself the opposite task and come up with fifty downsides. What happens if my investors don't deliver the funds? Which happened in this case. What happens if I get a major upset on planning? Which happened in this case. What happens if the cost estimates turn out to be wildly understated? Which happened in this case. What happens if the GDV turns out to be way lower than we're expecting? Which happened in this case. What happens if this project goes on for in excess of two, two and a half years, what's that going to do to my concentration and my ability to do good work on other things? Which happened in this case. So, you get my point. And then the final one, what happens if they all go wrong all together?

Now you've got a balanced view, you can see all the positives and you can see all the negatives. You can see all the upsides, you can see all the downsides. Now, and only now, should you think about making your decision. This is balance. If you don't balance yourself, the universe will. I'm not saying on your very first project, I'm just saying at some point balance will happen. Until you accept this, until you accept the need to go beyond what most people would call 'due diligence', you are likely to get some severe corrections. Due diligence is a trite phrase in my view. Doing the diligence that is due. Doing the research that one ought to. Well, that's the same as saying, do an average amount of diligence, do a typical amount of diligence, do enough to 'get you by' level of diligence. Whatever you do in terms of due diligence, if that's all you do, you're going to miss something. It's going to bite, sting, kick and hurt you badly.

So, what I suggest you do is follow my process, which I've called undue diligence, beyond due diligence. Please make sure that before you get involved in a project, especially a project of this size, that you conduct undue diligence. Just to make sure that as well as the upsides, which most people are very good at calculating, you've got a really firm understanding of all the downsides. Of course, this also goes the other way. If you naturally only tend to see the downsides, you need to stack up the upsides otherwise you will never make any projects.

We've talked about the property itself, we've talked about the team, we've talked about assumptions we've made, we've talked about the ten per cent rule and we've talked about doing undue diligence. Now moving on to the final lessons.

I think there are many things in this project that we did right, and I want to make sure that we share and remember those lessons. We certainly made the right decision to use a separate company, an SPV (Special Purpose Vehicle), specifically an LLP. That ringfenced all the liabilities, potential liabilities and potential future losses within that SPV. It didn't expose any of our personal assets or our other companies or other assets to any liability. These are known as contingent liabilities and they were avoided. The LLP specifically was the best choice of SPV, because it gave us so many advantages with capital allowances.

We also made the right decision to use professionals. This wasn't 'back of a fag packet' planning. We used professional surveyors, we used professional architects and we used professional quantity surveyors. All of these things ultimately go a long way to protecting not only the business case, but our reputations. What we didn't do was recklessly charge in. We did a lot of due diligence.

For all of us, reputation is important, in different ways. It's important for me to be able to hold my head up and say, 'Well, I did everything that could reasonably have been expected of me.' I'm not saying I ran the project to perfection. There's a level of difference between saying 'I could have done it better' and 'I did it wrong.' I do not believe this project went wrong. I believe this project was subject to a combination of unfortunate events, a perfect storm if you will. When any project is subject to a combination of events beyond your control, and beyond your expectation, it can falter.

Here is a really important lesson: fear. Fear is a reaction, courage is a decision. If you fear getting involved in these sorts of projects, you're certainly never going to make a mistake because you will not do them. Conversely, you're never going to make big returns on projects like this. 'The person that's never made a mistake has never made anything" is a quote often heard. Ultimately, the only perfectly safe way to do anything is to do nothing, then it can't possibly go wrong, can it? I'm proud of the fact that we tried. I'm proud of the fact that we persisted for two and a half years before ultimately accepting the fact that there was nothing else that we could do to make it work as the investors started repossession.

Failure cannot live with persistence. Although this project didn't turn out as we would have wanted it to, so many other things in our life did because we persisted. Yes, on social media we've got the haters. As Grant Cardone himself says, 'Unless you've got any haters, you're not actually doing anything, you're not known for anything.' I'm not saying that I want to be known only for the Paradigm project, but I do want to be known for what we do. What we do has a positive impact on so many people's lives, through Touchstone Education. For every hater, you're going to get several followers or fans. The more haters you get, the more followers you're going to get. The more followers you get, the more you can change people's lives. This is highly pertinent to myself, Aniko and everybody at Touchstone Education. We love what we do.

What else did we do right in this project? We made sure everybody had the correct legal advice. The LLP paid for it. I don't pretend to understand why the investors chose not to release their security in order to finish the project. Their security was on an asset that had been bought for £325,000, to remind you. What was offered to them instead were three things. First, a replacement of that security of £325,000 with £150,000 in cash and

£150,000 of personal guarantees. Secondly, they were offered an extremely viable route to get the project finished and to share in the positivity that I'm sure would have arisen as a result of finishing said project. Thirdly, which is the most important to me, is that what was on the table was reasonable. I'm not going to say fair, because fair is a perception that's personal. What's fair to one person will be completely unfair to another, which is why I prefer the word 'reason.' The logic demonstrated why we had got to where we had got to, the various steps that had been gone through and the proposed resolution. So, it was security replacement, it was a route to get the project finished, there was a rationale to it. It wasn't numbers plucked from the air.

Here's another thing that we did right. When we were challenged, when we were threatened with 'exposure' on social media, we stood firm. The threats the to 'expose' us were threats and bullying. The only way I know to deal with bullies is to stand up to them. That got me, personally, some haters, but ultimately, I think we did the right thing. I accept the outcome and as we grow, we take on more challenges.

During the same time that Paradigm was happening, we were building our HMO portfolio. We now have a substantial, by most people's reckoning, portfolio of HMOs. If worst came to worst, if we lost everything else for whatever reason, could we make a very nice living off the HMOs that we've got? Absolutely.

Why am I talking about HMOs in the context of Paradigm? I'm talking about HMOs as an example because we did numerous other property projects at the same time as Paradigm. We didn't have 'all of our irons in one fire' metaphorically speaking. We didn't allow the setbacks, the disappointments, the frustrations of dealing with Paradigm to stop us doing other things. We've got a very well-established property training business now. It really gives me, and I know it gives Aniko too, huge pleasure to see the thank you notes we receive and to see the comments that people make about how their lives have totally changed as a result of interacting with our company, Touchstone Education.

If we'd have buried our heads in the sand, if we'd have retreated, if we'd have said, 'Oh, this is all too much,' if we had given into the pressure, the HMOs, Touchstone and all our other businesses would never have happened. Another lesson I'd like to share with you is the importance of carrying on and not becoming totally consumed by one issue, by one setback. We all need to be bigger than that. None of us is ever going to have a perfect life, where absolutely nothing on our personal, physical, emotional, spiritual, familial, business or money life is not subject to challenge. In everything in life, we get equal measures of challenge and support. Just when you think you've got everything under control, that's the precise point that one of those plates stops spinning, falls on the floor and breaks. Whatever your biggest challenge in your life is, whatever you perceive it to be, I can guarantee you nobody else in the world sees it that way. 'Today's news is tomorrows fish and chip wrapper.'

I'm going to sum up our journey so far. I'm going to reflect on what is close to fifty years in property now (if I include my younger self scurrying about under the floor, ripping out lead and taking it to the scrap merchant) and I'm going to reflect on the next fifty years. What does the next fifty years in property look like for me?

I recently went to a medical appointment. I was getting checked out by the doctor. He didn't know me, it was the first time I had seen this particular doctor. It was a consultant surgeon and it was in connection with my Crohn's Disease. I've had Crohn's, since the age of fourteen. So this year, as I'm writing this book, I'm fifty-four and I'll have had Crohn's disease for forty years, which makes me one of the people in the UK that have had Crohn's Disease the longest. I'm perfectly fit. A bit overweight, but perfectly fit, strong and healthy. Good blood pressure, good heart and they can't find much wrong with me, apart from my Crohn's Disease.

So, this doctor asked me how old I was. I said, 'Well, Doctor, I'm about halfway through.' He said, 'What do you mean?' I said, 'Well, I'm roughly halfway through my life. I'm fifty-four years old, so I think I'm halfway through.' He looked at me, lowered his glasses down his nose, shook his head and said, 'I think you're being awfully optimistic, young man.' I just laughed at him. I didn't know what else to do. I carried on laughing but he wasn't reacting. So, I stopped laughing and said, 'You're serious, aren't you?' He said, 'Absolutely. I don't want you basing your life on the fact that you're going to live for another fifty years.' I said, 'Damn right, neither do I, I'm going to live a lot longer than that.' He looked at me genuinely puzzled and confused and said, 'But you've got Crohn's Disease.' I replied, 'I know. I'm not on any medication, I haven't had any surgery for the last twenty-odd years, what's the problem? Yeah, I've got Crohn's Disease.' I'm absolutely convinced and focused and know that I can manage my Crohn's Disease. Many people who contract Crohn's or similar believe what society tells them, they curl up in a ball and die.

I was offered Humira by transfusion on a biweekly basis. A day in hospital every two weeks for the rest of my life! Why? It would supposedly help keep my Crohn's Disease in remission.

Now it was my turn to be totally confused. I said, 'Doctor, but I don't have any symptoms.' 'Ah, yes, Mr Smith, but you never know what's bubbling beneath the surface.' I replied, 'All right. So, you're suggesting I put some carcinogenic, fabulously expensive product into me by transfusion twice a week. For the rest of my life I've got to give up one fourteenth of it to lying in a hospital bed being shot up with various drugs that are going to do me no good.' His view: 'No Mr Smith, they'll do you an enormous amount of good.' 'Really?' No wonder the NHS is in trouble. I've got no symptoms, I'm not complaining of anything and they still want to put me in a hospital bed once a fortnight for a day. I looked at the side effects of Humira on Google when I got home to confirm what I remembered: spontaneous heart failure, spontaneous kidney failure! I'm not saying it would've happened the next day, but I am saying it's a very unpleasant substance if you don't need it.

So, as we move into the final chapter, here are my thoughts about my next fifty years.

I want to encourage you to challenge the status quo. The system, in so many different ways, shapes and forms is broken. Whether we're talking about education, whether we're talking about finance, whether we're talking about the banking system, whether we're talking about miss-sold PPI insurance. Maybe we're talking about LIBOR (London Inter-Bank Offer Rate) rigging, maybe we're talking about mortgage securitisation, maybe we're talking about the political system or maybe we're talking about health.

I believe it's more important than it has ever been before to be totally clear about what you as an individual want. If the solution you're being presented with, be it a financial solution on a project, be it social media, be it a 'medical solution' (and I put that in heavy inverted commas and use the word advisedly), ultimately nobody is responsible for us except ourselves. I'll leave you to think on that, as you make your way to the next chapter.

Chapter Twelve: So Far, So Good

Thank you for coming with me on my journey from South Yorkshire, where it all began when I got involved with my father on our first property projects together. Then, I didn't know much about the property projects, other than me getting scrap metal in exchange for pocket-money – I used to spend my earnings in the newsagent near us. It was one of those old ones with the beautiful sweet jars all around the walls and the shop-keeper would have to go up and down on ladders to get to them.

I remember Dad encouraging me to go in there with my pocket-money. I'm sure you can imagine it, can't you? I'd go in with a threepenny bit or six-pence or a few of the big old pennies, and say to the shop-keeper, (this is what my Dad used to do when he was a kid), 'you got any broken biscuits?' The guy would say, 'Yeah,' get his ladders out, climb to the top and get the jar of broken biscuits and Dad would encourage me to say, 'Well, get them fixed then,' and run out the door. Dad used to think that was incredibly funny. There's only a certain amount of times you can do that to the same shop-keeper before he's going to associate a cheeky little rascal with copper red hair and a very tired, old, Second World War joke. Still makes me chuckle though.

My earliest associations with property, on a serious note, were very, very positive. I'm looking back now over half a century of being involved with property in various ways and I really want to give you some reference points as well as a summary. I want to give you a context for everything I say in this last chapter because, yes, of course, I've learned things. Yes, of course, things have gone 'wrong.' Nothing is ever going to go perfectly right under any scenario. There are always going to be things that could be improved but I think it's vitally important that we always put it in context.

What is the context in this case? Well it's true to say that in one way, shape or form I've been involved in property virtually my entire life. Dad would buy, refurbish, live in and ultimately 'flip" our home, a primary principle residence, a PPR. There would have been no capital gains tax. There had been no income tax. It was a great strategy. It was the only access to wealth that Mum and Dad ever had because they were both teachers. It's what made them most of their money, what paid for their holidays. They would earn more from property than they ever did for being teachers. That's the first thing that he taught me. Property, using the lessons provided in the right context, can be a very, very valuable tool in order to help you build wealth over time.

Property is multi-generational. I never had the good fortune to know my Great-Grandad, but both my Grandads, my Grandparents on both sides, the English one and the Irish one, both used and leveraged property and businesses in different ways. This is a multi-generational property strategy.

Property is not a 'one trick pony.'

There are many, many different ways in which you can benefit from property and property investment, as indeed I have. I guess, compared to my Father and my Grandfathers time, the difference in my generation is that it's now possible to read books on property investment and take courses and be educated, fast-tracking your learning process with regard to property investment. Short of writing the books and creating courses for themselves, it's not something that either my Grandads or Dad had access to. By the way, I'm not intentionally focusing on the difference between the genders here. I'm talking about my Father and my Grandfathers because they were the ones that did property, and right back in my Grandads' day, and my Father's day, I guess your gender, male or female, was more significant career-wise than it is today. I could not do any of what I do without the huge input that I get from my wife, Aniko. I'm an engineer, she's an accountant. I'm a bit more aggressive. She's a bit more conservative. We make a good team.

My two Grandmothers and my Mother were all homemakers and I don't say that in any way other than as a representation of what actually happened.

So, as I reflect on myself and my fifty-year journey, I don't think it's ridiculous to include what I learned in childhood. Whether it's running about under the floors of Victorian buildings, literally sometimes as there was only enough head height for me to do it or watching my English Grandad's pride and the way in which he talked about the achievement of having built his own bungalow which would go on to make him significant amounts of wealth. It conditioned me. It formed me. You could say it forged my expectations as to what was normal and how normal people behaved with regard to property and property investment. I think most people in the UK that would agree that property certainly can be a great investment if you hold it, or if you purchase it with the intention of holding it, for the next ten, twenty, fifty years even, making some cash-flow from it in the interim. Make sure you get yourself properly educated, get the knowledge and get proper support. As long as it cash-flows i.e. you're not paying for the privilege of keeping it, then your property is paying you. As long as you've got positive cashflow, however small, and you keep it for enough decades, it will create wealth for you. That's just the natural process of the difference between property price inflation and the devaluation of currency caused by general inflation.

If you want to learn more about working with me and about working with Touchstone to see how we could speed up, improve and help you learn from our mistakes then please do feel free to get in touch. I want you to be able to contact us and I want you to be able to ask us personally how we'll support you, and how our guidance, our knowledge, will be relevant to your property journey.

If I roll the clock forward to when I became an adult and look at how quickly I started investing in property myself, I was just eighteen years old when I bought my first property in London, and that's gone down through the generations. Becci, my eldest daughter, has got her own home, her own property, with her husband Kenny. They bought their first property when they were in their twenties. Jack, our oldest son, bought his first property when he was eighteen. He had his first investment property in his twenties. Ben, my middle son, is now in property full-time. I don't believe any of this is an accident. I have three other children but at the time of writing this book they're not yet adults, so I can't really give you a fair steer on where they're going to end up.

I have to say, I would be surprised if they ended up in conventional 'nine to fives' having gone to do a normal degree at university. Not that I decry that in any way. I would just be surprised if that's how it turned out, given what I've seen with my other children. Although the younger three are not yet adults, they obviously talk about their plans, what it is they'd like to do over the years. As I say, I don't judge, but I'll just be surprised if that's how it turned out.

So, how might Touchstone Education be able to help you with your education?

We've got a whole range of courses geared to individual needs and preferences and I just want to talk a little bit now about what property success has brought to me over the years.

I've shared with you Six of The Best projects that I've had challenges with, six biggest mistakes that I've made in property. What I haven't shared with you is the hundreds of projects that have gone swimmingly well, made lots of money and put me in a good position as an educator to be able to share both the "good" and the "bad" about property.

This book was nearly called "The Good, the Bad and the Downright Ugly in the Property World" because I've seen all extremes and I'm sure you've heard it said before, 'The person who's never made a mistake has never made anything.' I prefer it said this way: 'If you're not earning, you're learning.' You've heard me say that before, and this is the version I love the best. First you LEARN and then you remove your "L" plates and you're just left with EARN.
Okay, so what does our property portfolio look like fifty years on from

me being involved in helping out Dad with refurbishments on Victorian properties? It's been more than thirty-six years since buying my first home. In 2018 I was fifty-four, so that gives you a feel for how long ago I got my first property. My first investment property was when I was twenty-three, which is more than thirty years ago. I would say we've been seriously investing in property in a major way, as opposed to focusing on our 'careers', since 2003 or 2004, so that's been fifteen years. I think it's important to bear all those dates in mind, because if you commit yourself to a path of property investment and in a year's time you don't have the property portfolio we have, don't beat yourself up. This has been a long process for us and I often say to people that property is a get rich scheme, but it is not a get rich quick scheme. There are a number of elements to successful property investing. One of which is just time.

But the good news for anyone reading this book is that with the right support, with the right education, with the right skill-set and technical capabilities, with the right mindset, mentoring, masterminding and with the right friend-set and colleagues within the same programmes as you, what took me decades (because I didn't have any support infrastructure like that until very recently), will probably just take you a few years.

Is it okay to embark on a journey that would see you create some income within a year but then real, inter-generational wealth within two, three or four years? I would say, yes, and many people would see it as fair exchange to trade a year or two of their lives in order to fundamentally change the outcome of that life. I certainly would. I did. That was the choice I made.

So, in 2018 what does Paul and Aniko's property portfolio look like? Well, I won't go into too much detail because this is the summary. We've done the detail. I'm just going to give you an overview.

My first investment property was a quasi-HMO, but I didn't do very well as you've read earlier in this book. We now do it properly. We have an HMO portfolio that we own, mostly five beds, although we've got sixes and sevens too. Those HMO properties give us sixty-three HMO rooms.

The typical turnover for a month for our HMO properties is in excess of £24,000 and this element of our portfolio alone generates a completely passive income of many thousands of pounds a month. More on that shortly because many people say, 'Well, how can you have a completely passive income if you're managing HMOs? I've only got two and they're really hard work.' Well, hold that thought. Our HMO's typically cash-flow £8,500 per month and out Lettings business looks after them. Operationally we are not involved.

Imagine an element of your portfolio that is not managed by you is generating, let's say, £8,500 profit per month, multiply that by twelve and it is just over £100,000 per year. To have a minor element of our property portfolio generating six figures is, I think, pretty good. Despite the fact that some of our HMOs have given us some challenges and despite the fact that at the age of twenty-three this was precisely the property strategy that caused me pain, I didn't give up. I came back and learned how to do it properly. With all the changes to HMO legislation in October 2018, HMO investing has really grown up and it is a strategy for serious professionals now.

Our lettings company manages, at the time of writing over 200 HMO rooms. Where did they all come from if we only own 63 HMO rooms? Well, because we couldn't find an acceptable professional HMO management company, we started our own HMO lettings agency. To begin with that was painful and we had to subsidise the business, but we've done it. We've got a fantastic team and they do a brilliant job. We charge 15% management fee to manage other people's HMOs. If somebody offers to manage your HMO's for 6% to 10%, please don't let them because they won't be able to afford to do it properly. Could we potentially do it for 11% to 12% without losing money? Maybe, but it's that last 3% that gives us profit.

We're managing HMO rooms for other people and they turnover

around £50,000 per month. Our profit margin on that is between 3% and maximum 5%. The average is 4% by the time we've paid our team and the overheads. 4% of £50,000 is another £2,000 per month profit. Now, that on its own isn't going to change the world, but what it does do is pay for our personal HMOs to be managed completely hands-free. We've got a professional team doing it for us and it gives us a platform to manage HMOs for other people. In combination, with our HMO rent plus the management fees for other people, we will certainly be making in excess of £10,000 a month for the two together. But let's now just look at leverage and scale.

Given that we've got an HMO management company there's no reason at all why we shouldn't manage BTL as well, so we do. Given that we've got that skill-set, people on the ground, vehicles, an office and all the other infrastructure you need, there's no reason at all why we shouldn't have an estate agency as well, which we do. We're not there yet, but the business plans show a minimum of £5,000 growing quite quickly to £10,000 per month income from our combined lettings and estate agency business, looking after HMOs and single lets. Property is a long-term game. It's taken us more than three years to get to the point that our lettings/estate/single let/HMO agency is making that kind of money.

We're moving towards the end of this book, which I hope you've enjoyed and, more importantly, taken lessons from and made decisions about what to do with your future and property investing. Before we come to the end, I just want to reflect on the other parts of our property business; our property portfolio.

We still have a number of BTL, and although we think that BTL are very good, over the years we've found other ways in which to accelerate or increase the returns on investment, above normal BTL returns. BTL provide a regular, steady, monthly cash-flow. I always have to remind myself to be careful not to be dismissive about BTL. Ultimately, other advanced strategies may come and go as legislation and opportunity changes over the years but Buy-To-Lets for single familes are arguably the mainstay of any property portfolio. For this reason, although we may use some of our properties that were once BTL as, for example, Serviced Accommodation, we always make sure that the underlying asset, the property, will work as a BTL. A general tip that I'd like to share with everybody is that whatever you do with your property – SA, HMO's, lease options – if one of your exit routes in your investment plan is to always make sure it works as a BTL, you will have a far, far more secure business.

Coming back to the few BTL that we still have, why have we retained these? Well, not all properties will work as HMOs, or SA, or the other higher cash-flowing strategies. We've ended up with a few BTL and they perform extremely well as BTL's. I'm thinking, for instance, of an ex-local authority property that we have. It's actually a very nice ex-local authority property which we bought for £103,500 in late 2008.

It's in a nice area. In fact, so nice that the entire development is Grade III or Category C listed. An ex-local authority listed building! Local authority doesn't mean bad. The outside of the building has got many art nouveau features as that's the age that it's from. It's about a five-minute walk to the train station and it's in the town centre. Put all these things together and add to that the fact that it's a four-bed, and it's a very desirable place to live.

You can imagine that the mortgage payments on a £100,000 flat where we've got a £75,000 mortgage are tiny. It's an interest-only mortgage at two per cent. Well, this is the way I normally do the maths in my head. One per cent of £75,000 is £750 per year, therefore, two per cent is going to be £1,500 per year. Divide that by twelve and you get £125 pounds per month. The income from that flat, because it's a very desirable, large, four-bed, is £600. The normal calculation that I do is to deduct the twenty-five per cent for voids, maintenance, letting agent fees and the rest, which is £150 and that leaves £450. From that take the mortgage of £125 and you're left with £325. So, £325 a month conservative cashflow.

I say conservative cashflow because we've got a very well-established family tenant who has been there for years and is likely to be there for many more years. They've got children of school age and they need a four-bedroom house. In fact, where else are they going to get a four-bedroom house, a very nice place, for £600 a month in our area? It would be very hard. We've never done a refurbishment on it. We don't need to. When you get a lovely family in it like we've got, they will tend to do the refurbs themselves to keep it nice because they want to live long-term in a nice house.

So, that's £3,900 a year. If you'll forgive me a little rounding, let's call it £4,000 a year. Even if we tied up £25,000 of deposit, which we haven't, but that's a story for a different day, then your cash on cash return will be £25,000 tied up for £4,000 free cash flow after all costs per annum, which is 16%. Where else are you going to get 16% return on your capital? That completely ignores capital growth. I'm absolutely, one hundred per cent, for the record, not saying that BTL are bad. If we were to put that property on the market now we would enjoy some capital growth.

If we're conservative the capital growth over ten years is 50%. Another £50,000 of wealth created. Even if we had tied up £25,000 pounds to make this happen, we would have had that back twice over. Our equity in this property is £75,000 pounds and it delivers £4,000 pounds a year.

What else do we have? Well, for many years I've been investing my pension into commercial property. Pensions have a lifetime allowance of £1 million. So, what do you do with your reserves and your resources once you've fully invested your pension? This is a first world problem! Our net pension yield is 11%. Based on £1m lifetime allowance this is £110,000 per year which can be drawn from the age of 55.

Property has been, and continues to be, extraordinarily kind to us. I'm putting all this at the end of the book because I don't want anyone to be thinking, as a result of reading this book, that property is a minefield to be stayed away from. It's not. Property is the gift that keeps on giving.

But you need to know how to administer your property portfolio, how to encourage it to give you more, and how to avoid the pitfalls. You'll find many, many books on property wealth creation saying, 'Invest in property, it's easy, it's fantastic, you'll make millions.' Many people do, but some people also "lose their shirt" because they buy the wrong property at the wrong price or in the wrong way.

Make no mistake, my friends, I love property, but I don't love investing in property with a blindfold on. You've got to be fully awake. The reason I'm sharing these upsides now, is I've just given you a book pretty much full of downsides. I don't want you to leave this book thinking, 'Oh my God, I shouldn't ever invest in property,' because that is the one single biggest mistake you'll probably ever make in your life. Please, get the right support, get the right education, get the right knowledge and get the right mentors. They will help you do it so much faster.

If you like the idea of working with Touchstone, we'd love to work with you. If you like the idea of working with me personally, I would love to work with you.

What else do we have in our property portfolio? Well, we've also got a number of commercial properties outside of our pension schemes. We love commercial property so much, and we don't only love it as a vehicle that sits inside our pension schemes. Of course, there are additional advantages: tax-free income and the government giving your tax contributions back should you invest in a pension scheme, and many other reasons to invest in a pension, but that is not a set of reasons not to invest in commercial property outside a pension scheme too. Quite the opposite. We hold a number of very well-performing commercial property assets, offices and similar outside of our pension scheme as well. Not instead, as well.

We really do have a diverse and diversified property portfolio. What else do we have? Well, in addition to our HMOs, buy-to-lets and in addition to our commercial property, our shops and offices, in addition to our letting agency and our estate agency, many people know us for our serviced accommodation business. Taking relatively normal flats and houses you could easily use as a buy-to-let. We rent out to guests, not tenants, by the night, the week, or the month and not under a tenancy agreement but rather exactly the same way you would go and stay in a hotel or a guest house. You pay in advance by the night, using sites like Booking.com, Airbnb, LateRooms and all the others. That really is a fantastic business to be in.

I haven't concentrated on it overly much in this book but if it's serviced accommodation that you're interested in, then perhaps consider reading one of my other books, The Serviced Accommodation Success Manual. Thank you to everybody that's bought it and read it and for making it a number one Amazon best seller in all categories; I found I had to pinch myself a few times when that happened. A property investment book, not only that but a property investment book in a niche of property called Serviced Apartments, becoming a number one Amazon bestselling book in all categories. Amazing and thank you. I've had some lovely feedback from my readers. So, if serviced accommodations is your thing, or you want it to be, go get that book, read it and find out if serviced accommodation is for you.

Market Analysis for 2018 for Serviced Accommodation

Visit http://bit.ly/sabonus18 to profit from this strategy.

What else have we got in our property portfolio? The list just carries on. Well, books and book-writing. Many people say, 'Oh, you can't make any money from writing books.' You can. It's hard to make money from just selling books on Amazon but you can make good money if you're the author.

Passive income. Everything I do is geared at passive income, with one exception. That is what I'll come to last:

Touchstone Education

I know very well what my highest values are. My highest value is inspiring others to create wealth through knowledge with support. That's number one. By just offering you the chance to read this book, I'm not living my highest value. I need to do everything I can to support your learning journey, to help you to create wealth, to encourage you to read it. Only then am I living my highest value. Second highest value, creating wealth for myself and my family through business. Third highest value, my family. In that order. Inspiring others to create wealth for themselves, creating wealth for myself, and family. Those are my three highest values.

When you spend all your time living your highest value, you don't want it to be outsourced and automated. You want to do it yourself. I could get very involved in the project management, I could get involved in sourcing properties, I could get deeply involved in the finance side. I could do whatever I want with our businesses (I say 'whatever I want' although I'd have to get Aniko to agree that it was okay!) Aniko wouldn't stop me doing something that was in line with my highest values.

Imagine having a life where literally on a daily basis you get up and do what you want. What would you do? I'm recording this book, this is the way I "write" books. I think my transcribers do a great job, thank you, everybody. I just put my headset on and go out in all weathers. Sometimes it's hard for them to hear what I'm saying with howling gales or rain or various background noises. As I'm recording this particular piece of the end of this book, I'm in Portugal, in the Algarve. I'm looking out over a glorious lagoon on a beautifully sunny day. Not a cloud in the sky. To my left, I'm looking at multi-million pound houses that are being built and in front of me I've got a nature reserve. To the right of me, I've got a forest. I can see a man in a turquoise top with a lady with a rusty red dress on, walking two dogs. I can see a young girl with a grey vest and orange shorts running. I can see a young couple, a little bit too far away for me to give you a detailed description, riding bikes. People exercising in a gorgeous place. If I turn around I've got a car park behind me and there are two fabulous restaurants overlooking the lagoon. That's the environment I'm in whilst I'm "writing" this book for you. I'm sharing this with you because I want you to think, 'Where would I be on the perfect day for the rest of my life?' What's the temperature like? How does the sun feel on your skin? Who's around you?

What am I doing now? I'm walking back up to the villa that we've got in the complex that we're staying in. We're staying in Ayrton Senna De Silva Avenue, in a very nice, mostly owner-occupied complex. Swimming pools, gyms, massage centres, everything that you would need. Typically, what most people would need to make their life, to make their holiday, to make their retirement, whichever it is, very enjoyable.

I'm walking back up there now. In the next ten minutes I'll be there, and this book will be finished. As a family we'll sit down, we'll have breakfast together and we'll talk about what we're doing today. I know one of the things I'm doing today. I'll be re-writing some slides. I just want them to be better. It's never going to be perfect, but I want to try and improve them for a webinar that I'm doing tomorrow night. As it's my training business I can do it from anywhere in the world. All I need is a laptop and a decent internet connection.

I've got some calls today, not many, two, with a couple of key business partners today. I'm going to be spending the vast majority of the day with Aniko, my wife, and my two youngest children, Jenny and Jude. I quite like getting up early so probably when I get back to the villa the three of them will still be in bed. They won't have missed me, hopefully. I like getting up early, going out for walks, getting my head straight, thinking about things and working on projects in my head. But, to be very specific, when you merge your passion with your profession, when you make your vacation your vocation, you're going to build yourself a life that you don't need a holiday from. Someone is going to tell you, 'You need to take a break,' and you're going to tell them, 'No, I don't. I'm doing the thing that I was born to do,' whatever that is. I'm perfectly relaxed. I'm having a wonderful time. I couldn't do anything to relax myself more, because this is the thing I want to do the most.

Literally build yourself a life that you don't need a break from. That's my life, in the training, education, and inspiration space. I've learned over the last few years to serve more people and genuinely add value to their lives. What do I do? I help them to financial and time freedom. Are they willing to pay for that? Of course they are. Who wouldn't pay me any price I mentioned, as long as the people that I work with actually become financially and time free? Who wouldn't make the decision to invest in themselves and their future? Yeah, they're going to have to do some work. They're going to have to work hard for twelve or eighteen months, but for the rest of their lives they can then do whatever they want.

Most people, if they're lucky, get to go abroad and "live the dream" for two weeks a year. What does that mean? To get to "live the dream" for one year takes them twenty-six years? That's twenty-six years at two weeks per year, isn't it? Maybe, over a fifty-year working life, the combination of those experiences might total to two years.

Or, get your head down, work hard, work with me for the next twelve to eighteen months and every waking moment of every single day for the rest of your whole life is complete and absolute financial time freedom. You can be doing "the thing" that you love to do. So, not only would you then enjoy those years of your life far more fully and in a deeper way than you otherwise could, caring far more for those about you than you're otherwise going to be able to, but you're also, probably, going to have far more of them.

How many people do you know that are being put into an early grave because of stress, financial worry, a boss that they hate, workplace politics, whatever it is? Far, far too many people on the planet go far too early, having only lived to a fraction of their potential. I live in Scotland. I am not

Scottish. Scotland has a national hero, William Wallace. One of his sayings was, 'Everyone dies, but not everybody truly lives.' Life, your life, my life, is a very perilous proposition. I'll tell you how perilous. Life is so dangerous that nobody gets out alive! That's slightly tongue in cheek. It's not only a question of enjoying the years that you have far more fully and to a greater extent but having far more of them. That's my objective. I want to help to get you to that place.

Thousands of people that I've worked with over the years, from a wealth, business and property education perspective, have supported my ideals and have invested in themselves. So, to my closing thoughts in this book. If you like the idea of property, property investment, financial freedom, financial security and time freedom, what are you prepared to do to get it? If you want to discuss the options, if you want to discuss how you could take your journey forward, get in touch www.bit.ly/portfoliocall. Let's see how we can support your journey. I wish you very well, my friends. I hope to see each and every one of you sometime very soon. Thank you for reading this book. You've all been wonderful, and I've been Paul. Bye, bye.

Will You Leave a Book Review?

Did you enjoy this book and was it useful? I will be very grateful when you post a short review and your success story on Amazon right now!

Your support makes a difference and *we read and respond to all the reviews personally* with Aniko to make this book even better!

To leave a review right now, go here: https://amzn.to/2Mg54fL